Steam Railways in Colour
AROUND NORTHAMPTONSHIRE

Frontispiece. 'Can I come up onto the footplate please?' How many times has that question been asked at platform ends during the good old steam days? A little schoolboy has the driver straining out of his cab listening to his request whilst probably the most famous of all steam locomotives, A3 class Pacific No. 4472 FLYING SCOTSMAN, brews up ready for departure at Banbury station on 2 May 1990. *(Joe Rajczonek)*

STEAM RAILWAYS IN COLOUR
AROUND NORTHAMPTONSHIRE

by

RICHARD COLEMAN and JOE RAJCZONEK

W. D. WHARTON
Wellingborough

First published in 1993 by
W.D. Wharton
37 Sheep Street
Wellingborough
Northamptonshire NN8 1BX

ISBN 0 9518557 2 7

Designed and typeset by John Hardaker, Wollaston, Northamptonshire
Printed and bound in Great Britain by
Butler & Tanner Ltd
Frome, Somerset

ACKNOWLEDGEMENTS

We are indebted first and foremost to all the photographers who have so willingly allowed us access to their priceless colour transparencies, and for all their assistance with caption information. Also to the Northampton branch of the RCTS for the loan of the late Sid Bellham's photographs with the kind permission of Mrs Bellham. Likewise, our grateful thanks to Mrs Locke for the loan of her late husband's photographs with the help of RCTS member Ron Gammage, to whom we also offer our thanks. In addition we have received much appreciated co-operation from Ron White of Colour Rail.

Thanks are also expressed to Ken Fairey, Les Hanson, Ross Smith, Barrie Taylor, Ian Wright, and especially to Graham Onley and Robin Puryer for all their additional help with information for our needs. Our special thanks go to Tony Haylock for his photographic assistance and expertise in producing colour prints from the many slides selected, and for his help in keying captions onto disk. Thanks, too, to Mrs Carol Roberts for typing assistance.

We would also like to thank Don Breckon for writing the foreword, for his sketch and for providing a transparency of his latest painting commissioned by Mr and Mrs John Rowell, to whom we are very grateful for allowing it to be reproduced in this book.

Finally, our many thanks to the production team – John Hardaker for his continuing patience in face of our numerous requests to alter and amend our original layout and manuscript; Mick Sanders for answering our incessant questions about printing techniques; and finally Robert Wharton who has given us great freedom in the preparation of the book.

Half title caption
The signalbox at Neilsons in Wellingborough creates a ghostly image in foggy conditions. *(Joe Rajczonek)*

Title page caption
The once familiar headboard that adorned the front of a Northampton Black 5 locomotive for certain special football trains is shown in its full glory on the front of No. 45398. It is Saturday 2 March 1964 and the Cobblers are away to Swindon Town. *(David Pick)*

CONTENTS

'CALLING AT KETTERING'
by Don Breckon

'Jubilee' class 4-6-0 No. 45684 'JUTLAND' arriving at Kettering with a northbound express in 1964. Among the passengers and railway staff are boys from Kettering Grammar School, having a morning's 'train-spotting' on the station. *(Painting reproduced courtesy of Mr and Mrs John Rowell)*

FOREWORD
by Don Breckon

Kettering station was the place where my real interest in trains and railways began. For a boy from Corby in his first term at Kettering Grammar School, the station was a magnet. Allowed out of the school gates for half-an-hour at lunchtime, my friends and I were off down the hill, pausing only to tip our caps in the approved manner to any masters we might meet on the way.

The reason for our eagerness was that two express trains were due in this period, one southbound and one northbound. With luck they would be headed by one of the Jubilee class engines which carried nameplates. It was the 'namers' which interested us, and if it was a good day at least one would be a 'cop' to be neatly underlined in our *Ian Allan ABC of LMS Locomotives* when we got home later that evening.

The station had an atmosphere of travel and faraway places which we found exciting – impressive awnings, five platforms, a subway and refreshment room. Corby had nothing like this. Arriving on the centre platforms we studied the signals for advance news of any arrivals, and then the first of the expresses would come coasting round the curve north of the station, sweeping through the platforms and disappearing towards London. 'Keyes again', or 'Tyrwhitt' or 'Wemyss' – we couldn't even pronounce some of the names on the engines!

Then there was the northbound train which stopped at Kettering, but our time was limited and if it was late it meant a mad run up the hill to the school where a prefect would be waiting at the gate with the detention book – and he was collecting names too! Most days we made it, and I remember an image as we glanced back on leaving the station which has stayed with me of a black Jubilee standing at the head of its train surrounded with swirling smoke.

Later a group of us started to cycle to Glendon Junction which became our weekend train spotting location. It was the traditional long summer day on a grassy embankment, notebooks, bottles of *Tizer* and *Oxo* tins packed with sandwiches – 'I'll swap you an egg sandwich for a meat-paste one.' Some of the Jubilees were in BR green livery by now, which enhanced their appearance and our enthusiasm for them. We grew restless, however, when we looked at photographs of the Pacific locomotives of the West Coast main line, and finally decided that we would cycle the 25 miles to Blisworth to see the real thing. It was well worth while, but there was so much cycling involved that gradually this became our main interest! Eventually we put our railway books away and joined the Rockingham Forest Wheelers.

An interest in railways may fade but it never really goes away, through the years of National Service, Art College and teaching I was always stirred by the sight and sound of trains. As an Art teacher in Reading in the 1960s I saw the gradual disappearance of steam from the old GWR territory – a depressing situation. The ex-GWR locomotives, in particular the 'Castle' class, had reawakened my old enthusiasms and I started buying railway books and magazines again. Strangely it was back in Northamptonshire that I was to see the last of some GWR engines, and this was a turning point in my career as an artist, changing the subject matter of my paintings which previously had never featured the railway scene. Driving up to Corby for the weekend I passed the site of the old Cransley

Iron Works, and there to my amazement were rows of obviously GWR locomotives! I concentrated on the road with some difficulty. The following morning was very cold with a light dusting of snow, but my brother and I went over for a look around what we discovered to be Cohen's yard where steam engines were being cut up for scrap.

Cohen's Yard

Don Breckon

It was a sad sight. I sketched and photographed lines of locomotives, including three of the Grange class, and went away feeling helpless and dismayed that these splendid engines were to be reduced to lumps of metal the following day.

At that time my paintings were semi-abstract in style and approach. I began to work on a new series based on the shapes observed in the locomotive scrapyard. These were my first paintings on a railway theme, but before long the feeling of wanting to portray the engines as they should have been grew stronger and I moved away from an abstract approach to scenes of steam locomotives in the landscape.

Now the paintings were trying to bring the past to life, reviving memories for myself and, happily, for others. A time machine for the imagination, perhaps, which started in a Northamptonshire scrapyard.

With these strong memories of my own childhood days spent in the pursuit of trains, it was disappointing that North-amptonshire did not seem to feature often among the many and varied books of railway photography. This was remedied on a grand scale in 1987 when Richard Coleman and Joe Rajczonek's book *Steam Nostalgia Around Northampton* was published. The high standard of quality photographs, captions and layout made for a memorable book.

Followed by *Steaming into Northamptonshire* (1988) and *Railway Images Around Northamptonshire* (1992) the series proved that there was indeed an excellent store of railway photographs to draw from in the county.

Now Richard and Joe have brought together a collection of colour photographs for their fourth book, one which recalls the rich variety of the railway past of Northamptonshire. Even for those of us who know the locations there are unfamiliar images which will add greatly to the pleasure and enjoyment of our memories.

Don Breckon

1993

INTRODUCTION

Following our very successful trilogy of books depicting the county's railway using black and white photographs we received many letters of praise and encouragement for yet more material to be published. Could we possibly follow this with something different yet still on the theme of steam nostalgia in the county? Talk of a colour book prompted us to approach our ever-faithful band of local railway photographers in a search for colour transparencies.

It must be remembered that local railway photographers took pictures of the steam railway scene, as it then existed, for their own personal record, with little thought that their work may one day be viewed by an audience wider than their fellow local enthusiasts. Consequently most used black-and-white film because it was not only cheaper but had more exposure latitude, therefore enabling more successful photographs to be taken. Fortunately, though, some also attempted colour photography, but this wasn't as straightforward as it is nowadays. Not only was colour film expensive, but to obtain good results, especially of trains at speed, a good quality camera with a high shutter speed was essential. Exposure was critical and this resulted in many photographers having problems with over- or under-exposed transparencies.

Also, unknown to the photographer at the time, some makes of colour film were to suffer badly in storage over the next 30-35 years, resulting in colours fading significantly on the transparencies. However, despite all this, we have been able to select a good cross-section of quality transparencies showing a wide range of railway subjects in and around the county. The best of the work of some 20 local photographers therefore presents a fascinating and rare colour record of all the final years of steam working on main lines and branch lines, including the forgotten ironstone byways. Most of the photographs were taken between the late 1950s and the late 1960s, and feature some 35 different classes of engine.

The county town and immediate area is prominent, and a chapter is devoted to this area. The rest of the county is basically split in two, and two more chapters deal with each of these sections. The final chapter is left to the ironstone railways which were largely unnoticed by many enthusiasts, but nevertheless formed an important part of the steam railway in the county. Many of the scenes throughout the book can never now be repeated, and it is hoped that some pleasant memories will be stirred by the illustrations portrayed. The different styles of photography have helped to show not only traditional views of locomotives but also trains at night, in the snow and in the landscape; and they are all in full colour.

To retain the theme of using the work of local contributors, we are very pleased to include a recently commissioned new painting by Don Breckon. Born in Corby, Don is a railway artist of high repute who spent many hours of his youth train-spotting at Kettering station and Glendon Junction. His love of steam is so vividly illustrated in his paintings, and we are sure readers will agree that the inclusion of his latest painting adds that special something to this book.

Every steam enthusiast longs to relive the good old days. An impossible dream, perhaps, but the imagination knows no bounds, and the feast of full-colour pictures presented here is waiting to transport you back in time. Sit back and enjoy the ride!

Richard Coleman and Joe Rajczonek

STEAM AROUND NORTHAMPTON TOWN

1. It is the last Saturday in August 1963 and the annual excursion to Derby Locomotive Works for the railway enthusiasts of the area has come round again. Stanier class 5 No. 45302, a favourite of Northampton loco shed where it was kept in good clean external condition, stands ready to depart from Northampton Castle's platform 1. Although it is initially facing the wrong direction for Derby it will travel via Wellingborough and Kettering which will set it on course to run right through, this being the only regular working of the year for a Northampton engine and crew with Derby as their destination. The gloom on the platforms still requires the gas lamps to be lit. *(Robin Puryer)*

2. With cylinder cocks open Stanier Coronation Pacific No. 46256 SIR WILLIAM A. STANIER, F.R.S. makes a steamy departure from Northampton Castle station on Saturday 14 July 1962 with the 9.05 a.m. Llandudno to Euston train. This train was one of the few expresses that called at Northampton. The external condition of the Coronation shows up superbly in the damp cloudy conditions more familiar to February than July! 46256 and 46257 were constructed after Sir William Stanier retired from the L.M.S., and his successor, H.G. Ivatt, introduced various design modifications to these fine locomotives, one of which was to fit Timken roller bearings to the axleboxes in place of white metal bearings as used on the rest of the class. The 'Duchesses', 'Coros' or 'Semis', as they were locally known, were probably the most liked class of locomotive seen at Northampton. *(Neville Simms)*

3. Platform 4 at Castle station and Northampton No. 1 signalbox stands proud as Standard class 2MT No. 84008 takes water on another overcast summer Saturday, 3 August 1963. Whilst the fireman regulates the water column the driver adjusts the injector and watches the overflow before the Wellingborough-bound train is ready for departure. In the background more steam is visible in the carriage sidings. (Roger West)

Steam Around Northampton Town

4. The photographer was fortunate enough to be friendly with the signalman in Northampton No. 1 signalbox and was able to gain access for a signalman's eye view of proceedings. From the signalbox window, on Sunday 20 July 1958, we see Stanier Black 5 No. 45035 with the 8.50 a.m. stopping train from Euston, rolling down the gradient past the refuse destructor plant, heading for Northampton Castle's platform 7. *(Ross Smith)*

5. An early summer's morning during August 1962 and the main line trains have been diverted via Northampton yet again as rebuilt Royal Scot No. 46115 SCOTS GUARDSMAN hurries past No. 2 signalbox and through Castle station with a Manchester to Euston express. The strong summer sunlight shows up the well-burnished paintwork on 46115 to good effect as a blustery south-westerly wind sweeps away steam from the safety valves and bends the tops of the poplar trees on the perimeter of Victoria Park. Fortunately 'Scots Guardsman' survived after the end of steam on British Railways, being purchased for preservation, and has since been out on the main line hauling special trains. *(Sid Bellham)*

6. A superb winter's day at Castle station with locally shedded Fowler 4P class tank No. 42353 basking in the sunshine. The black paintwork on the locomotive contrasts vividly with the red on the ex-works Brake Third coach numbered M27912M. To the left Northampton No. 2 signalbox stands to the north of the platform with another column of steam in the distance suggesting another train is shortly due on this Saturday 7 January 1961. The locomotive was based at Northampton from December 1957 to June 1962 before being transferred to Bangor. *(Brian Denny)*

Steam Around Northampton Town

7. The gas lamps and their corresponding reflections on the wet platform are the only bright spots on this dull, wet and miserable morning of 23 February 1964 as Northampton Castle station welcomes a Carlisle to Euston parcels, headed by Stanier Pacific No. 46248 CITY OF LEEDS. A bold attempt by the photographer to show that photographically steam trains *did* run in poor weather conditions. *(David Pick)*

8. The train was very long and heavy and, having pulled up at platform 1, 46248 then had to pull forward onto the River Nene overbridge so that the rear vehicles reached the platform for loading and unloading. From this position on the bridge the driver patiently awaits the signal to proceed southwards towards Roade. The name 'City of Leeds' was also carried by another in this class, No. 6244, from July 1940 to April 1941. *(David Pick)*

9. Glasgow (Polmadie) Stanier Pacific No. 46230 DUCHESS OF BUCCLEUCH eases out of Castle station and heads for Euston via Blisworth with a diverted Anglo-Scottish express on the cold but clear afternoon of Tuesday 24 April 1962. Tight curves, situated each side of the canal bridge near the loco shed, necessitated a severe speed restriction for locomotives of this size when taking this route to London. The siding in the foreground was gated and gave access to a petrol distribution depot in St James Mill Road. *(Ron Gammage)*

STEAM AROUND NORTHAMPTON TOWN

10. This photograph could be entitled 'Your Life in Their Hands', for the signalman in Northampton No. 1 signalbox assured the photographer that he *could* stand in this position, and that 'The Ulster Express' *would* be taking the through line towards Roade and *not* Blisworth. All the same, it was very unnerving as rebuilt Royal Scot No. 46170 BRITISH LEGION came under West Bridge with her driver opening the regulator as 140 tons of locomotive and tender swung across the points heading for the 1 in 200 incline towards Roade on Sunday 14 June 1959. *(Ross Smith)*

11. BR Standard 4-6-0 class 4 No. 75039 arrives from its home shed of Bletchley with the 5.28 p.m. stopping train to Northampton. The local draws into riverside platform 7 at 6.06 p.m. with the last of the sun's rays catching the underside of the station canopy on the evening of Tuesday 27 March 1962. The Standard 75039 had only recently been transferred from Chester, and stayed at Bletchley until May 1963 when it went to Derby. It may be better remembered as one of the engines to spend its last days at Tebay, banking trains up the Shap incline in 1967. (Ron Gammage)

12. There was often a good chance of seeing either a 'Patriot' or 'Jubilee' on the 5.55 p.m. from Northampton to Euston (5.06 p.m. ex-Rugby), and so it turned out on a cold spring Monday, 14 April 1958. Hauled by No. 45539 E.C. TRENCH the 'Patriot' is about to depart from Castle station's platform 1 and head for the metropolis with the last rays of the day's sunshine beaming down on it. (Ross Smith)

13. A red Northampton Corporation bus crosses Westbridge overlooking Castle station as Ivatt tank No. 41225 stands in platform 5 with the 4.10 p.m. train to Wellingborough on Saturday 2 May 1964. Remarkably this is the final day of service on this route and not one passenger is noticeable on the platforms. Such is the enthusiasm for steam in this day and age that if the same event was taking place it's unlikely one would be able to get near the train, let alone photograph it! *(Trevor Riddle)*

STEAM AROUND NORTHAMPTON TOWN

14. As the numbers of new diesel and electric locomotives entering service during the early 1960s became a flood, steam locomotives which in their hey-day were distinctly 'top link', were to be found on increasingly mundane duties. An example of this down grading came to light during the winter on 1963/64. Lengthy parcel trains, one in each direction, which were booked to ply their trade at Northampton Castle station every Sunday morning, found themselves promoted from the hitherto usual Stanier class 5 haulage to the regal provision of Stanier's Coronation Pacific No. 46235 CITY OF BIRMINGHAM, which is shown entering Castle station with a northbound parcels on a dismal 5 April 1964. The viewpoint of this photograph is unusual. How many local folk can remember the temporary 'open air' footbridge placed halfway along the platform during re-building of Castle station for electrification? Neither this nor its replacement could match the character of the original footbridge, hard up against West Bridge the top doors of which could be opened to disgorge excursionists onto the road to walk home or catch the usual late night Corporation buses to all parts of the town (see picture 12). *(Graham Onley)*

15. Adjacent to Northampton's Castle station stood the magnificent goods warehouse constructed at the same time as the station in 1881. Here is a rare glimpse inside during the final years of use before it was needlessly pulled down to make way for the inevitable car park space after 105 years in use. Dishwashers from Italy having arrived in through ferry vans are unloaded destined for Phillips Electrical at Sywell, while cartons of raisins, currants and sultanas are stored ready for delivery to Whitworths of Wellingborough. Just a small sample of the many goods that were handled which no doubt are transported on the road today. *(John Harrison)*

16. The large wooden sign situated above the entrance to the warehouse warning locomotive drivers not to take their engines inside. *(Joe Rajczonek)*

STEAM AROUND NORTHAMPTON TOWN

17. 'Steam' at Northampton Castle station platform 7 on Friday 1 January 1965. Steam from the train's heating system leaks from the coaches and merges into the station lights as D287 pauses on the 6.55 p.m. Euston to Birmingham. The train in question had run on similar timings for many years and was one of the few Euston to Birmingham/Wolverhampton services that continued to run during the ravages of the pre-electrification period. Alas the entire scene, the parcels pens, station canopies and even the old style black platform surfaces would be consigned to history within months leaving only the locomotive to linger on for a few more years. *(Graham Onley)*

18. Well aware that a nocturnal New Year's Day photograph of Northampton shed under steam in 1965 would never again be possible, the photographer decided to venture out in the bitter cold and try his luck. Remarkably, without the use of a tripod, he has produced a stunning photograph. The shed was reasonably well occupied in what was then a normal working day. Had it been more full there would have been insufficient light pouring from inside the shed. Standard class 5 No. 73048 from Nuneaton shows a red lamp to the front. It would have come onto the shed tender first to Bridge Street signalbox, the light of which can be seen to the lower right of the large light mass. 21 hours before this photograph was taken the New Year would have been heralded by the traditional sound of all available locomotives whistling for the last time. New Year's Eve at Far Cotton has never been the same since. *(Graham Onley)*

19. Local enthusiasts and railway photographers who regularly visited Northampton's shed on Sunday mornings were usually not too surprised to find a visiting locomotive from the more distant parts of the country, but this particular find was something different. B1 class 4-6-0 No. 61257 had arrived from Thornaby shed in the North Eastern Region and not only was it one of the rarest of all visitors but one of the dirtiest. Not only this but No. 61257 was announcing its presence before it was actually seen by producing an acrid yellow-grey smoke which filled the shed with a distinctive tar-like aroma which spread to the yard outside. Reminiscent of burning soot, it could even be smelt in neighbouring Henley Street and Rickard Street! As the locomotive was totally enclosed by other locomotives the only way the photographer could take a picture was to get into the cab of an adjacent locomotive. Also on this particular Sunday, 13 January 1963, Coronation Pacific No. 46220 CORONATION and Britannia Pacific No. 70014 IRON DUKE were on shed. *(Robin Puryer)*

20. A wander around the shed on Sunday 11 March 1962 shows a Hughes/Fowler 'Crab' No. 42786 from Nuneaton simmering next to Fowler 4P tank No. 42353, a local resident, on a beautiful early spring day. Of note is the old BR emblem on the tender of the 'Crab' as well as the early BR style non-standard front number plate with the closed 6 instead of the latter open 6. 42353 was a Northampton allocated locomotive from December 1957 to June 1962. *(Brian Denny)*

21. Christmas Day morning at Northampton shed in 1962 and all is quiet with not one locomotive in steam, as was customary on this day; and the shed more full than usual as hardly any trains were operating. The bitterly cold weather is illustrated by the frost on the sleepers even though the morning sun is shining brightly, and on the canal the thick ice that has built up over the previous few days has been broken up by a passing narrow boat the day before. Amongst all the local Stanier design ex-LMS locomotives, indigenous to this area, can be seen an ex-LNER 'B1' 4-6-0 No. 61204, a visitor from March shed, second from left. Sadly the days of walking round a packed steam shed at Northampton before Christmas lunch have faded into history. *(Robin Puryer)*

22. A look inside Northampton shed on Sunday 12 April 1964 finds Jubilee class 4-6-0 No. 45556 NOVA SCOTIA from Crewe North at rest on No. 1 road in commendably clean condition for the time. Fortunately the shed was unusually empty that morning and, without a locomotive in No. 2 road, the photographer has managed to obtain a particularly pleasing study of the locomotive with the shed lights reflecting off the green paint of the cab and tender. That day proved particularly rewarding for anyone in search of green 'namers', as Jubilee class No. 45655 KEITH, and two Britannias – No. 70021 MORNING STAR and 70023 VENUS – were also on shed. Quite a gathering of express steam power. (Graham Onley)

STEAM AROUND NORTHAMPTON TOWN

23. A late afternoon stroll around Northampton shed on Sunday 21 January 1962 shows an almost black Stanier Jubilee No. 45740 MUNSTER resting in between duties by the shed wall. On the smokebox door the locomotive carries the distinctive sign of its home shed at Aston in Birmingham. During this latter era of steam at the shed, Aston 'Jubilees' and 'Britannias' were regular visitors. *(Brian Denny)*

24. It was not every Sunday that an acceptably clean Britannia Pacific was to be seen alongside the coaling plant at Northampton shed. On 12 April 1964 the first sight of the locomotive would have been from the footbridge by the Bridge Street Junction signalbox en route to the shed. No doubt the shout of 'Brit on Shed!' would have crossed the lips of local train-spotters as they approached the shed. On this day the main part of the shed was not even half full, with several locomotives parked elsewhere – no doubt because the shedmaster had not exercised his shed-setting skills. This particular Britannia No. 70021 MORNING STAR, based at the time at Willesden, started its working life on the Western Region but was transferred to the Midland Division of the London Midland Region during 1957. The Standard class 4 No. 75054, seen buffered up to 70021, was an unusual visitor at the time. Whilst this type had occasionally been seen 'on the shed' they were most often seen hauling Euston suburban trains to Bletchley, Northampton and Rugby. *(Graham Onley)*

25/26. A glimpse through the broken fence by the canal side at Northampton shed shows the fireman preparing Stanier class 5 No. 45134 for work, while Britannia Pacific class No. 70011 HOTSPUR stands waiting to come out of the shed on Saturday 2 January 1965. After a while, with the sun dropping fast and little available light, the polished smokebox door of 70011 reflects the orange glow from the sun as the loco moves out of the shed.

After the barring of the use of some of the ex-LMS express locomotives from operating south of Crewe from 1 September 1964, the largest express locomotives to be seen in the area were the Standard BR Britannia Pacifics. Even so, the sighting of a Britannia on shed as late in local steam history as this date was approaching the unusual. Another unusual point about this particular locomotive is the fact that it is still carrying its nameplates.

By this date, although the volume of steam on view had much diminished, the range of loco sheds represented had tended to widen, and a visit to the shed by a Carlisle Kingmoor engine at that time would not have induced the elation that a similar visit as recently as three years previously would have done. Stanier class 5 No. 45134 had long been a habitué of the area, and was a Northampton allocated engine between January 1962 and the closure of the shed in September 1965. It was later to survive in service at Carnforth until the end of official BR steam in August 1968. *(both pictures Graham Onley)*

27. Northampton shed on Wednesday 21 December 1960 and most of the locomotives have already dispersed on their various rostered duties. A few remain, however, and as the roar of safety valves fills the air the unmistakable form of a Baby Scot (Patriot class) comes into view as No. 45533 LORD RATHMORE backs away from the yard, having been turned on the shed turntable ready for the trip back to its home shed of Rugby. At the end of December 45533 was transferred to Nuneaton shed, and appeared at Northampton in a much more presentable external condition on 7 January 1961 when it hauled a football special along the Bedford branch to Luton. *(Brian Denny)*

28. From the excellent vantage point of the footbridge linking Main Road in Far Cotton with the locomotive shed Thompson B1 class 4-6-0 No. 61204 gently negotiates the sweeping bend between Duston North Junction and Bridge Street Junction with the 12.28 p.m. Northampton Castle to Peterborough East train on Saturday 28 February 1959. The signalbox at Duston North Junction is visible on the right hand side of the picture. The footbridge and Bridge Street Junction signalbox can be seen in illustration 29 opposite. *(Ron Gammage)*

Steam Around Northampton Town

29. A quite splendid sight on Boxing Day 1960 at Bridge Street Junction signalbox as Stanier class 5 No. 45094 accelerates towards Bridge Street station with the 12.28 p.m. Northampton Castle to Peterborough East special. The weather could not be better, with a clear blue sky and cold conditions producing a fine exhaust from the locomotive at this rarely photographed location. Part of the locomotive shed can just be seen behind the signalbox. The same train was to be powered by a pair of class 5s in the following three years, but on this occasion 45094 managed admirably without assistance. (Brian Denny)

30. Standard tank No. 84008 in superb external condition stands in Northampton Castle's bay platform No. 5 on a glorious September's afternoon in 1963 ready to depart with a Wellingborough push-pull service. Northampton No. 1 signalbox casts its shadow over the front end of 84008 as the black smoke from the chimney indicates the fireman has placed a few shovels full of coal around the firebox in preparation for departure time, although with the signals remaining at danger this would not seem to be imminent. *(Sid Bellham)*

STEAM AROUND NORTHAMPTON TOWN

31. Britannia class Pacific No. 70047 sets off up the bank out of Northampton Castle station with the 8.46 a.m. train to London during a Saturday in September 1963. For some unknown reason this particular 'Britannia' was the only one of the 55 in the class never to be allocated a name. This train became a regular one for local train-spotters to catch to Roade or Castlethorpe, or even London during the last years of steam. Whenever a 'Brit' was on the early duty the spotters would travel in the first coach, open the windows in the compartment, and as Hunsbury Hill tunnel was approached the never-to-be-forgotten sound of the chime whistle would echo as the engine entered, and then steam, smoke and smuts would fill the compartment as the engine worked through the tunnel. As the train left the tunnel all the windows would be closed so that the atmospheric conditions inside the compartment could be savoured for a bit longer. Happy days indeed! *(Ken Clements)*

32. The totem and flower garden at the much lamented Bridge Street station at noon on 19 June 1960. *(Tommy Tomalin)*

33. In the bright winter morning sunlight of 31 December 1960 Northampton-based Fowler 4F class 0-6-0 No. 44239 opens up as it passes over the level crossing and through Bridge Street station with a Cotton Yards to Down Sidings inter-yard freight, known locally as the 'trip'. This magnificent station, the first in Northampton, was built by the London and Birmingham Railway in 1854 on its through route from Blisworth to Peterborough. 44239 remained a Northampton engine until June 1962 when it was transferred to Warrington. *(Brian Denny)*

STEAM AROUND NORTHAMPTON TOWN

34/35. The 12.28 p.m. train from Northampton Castle to Peterborough East makes a brief stop at Bridge Street station to pick up the odd passenger on Saturday 14 April 1962. Headed by B1 class 4-6-0 No. 61095, which has been fitted with a self-weighing tender, the train pulls away past the signalbox towards Hardingstone Junction and between all the once familiar landmarks that have now disappeared. Bridge Street station closed in 1964 and was quietly demolished in 1970, so removing every trace of this piece of Northampton's railway heritage. *(both pictures Ron Gammage)*

NORTHAMPTON
BRIDGE STREET LEVEL CROSSING

STEAM AROUND NORTHAMPTON TOWN

36. Wellingborough shed's recently acquired Ivatt tank No. 41224 in spotless condition whisks its two coach motor set through Bridge Street station, hauling the 12.20 p.m. train from Northampton Castle to Wellingborough Midland Road on Saturday 14 April 1962. A British Railways parcel van and bus stand in the station yard. The bus belonged to the Engineering Department and was used for taking the relaying gang to site locations that were inaccessible by train. *(Tommy Tomalin)*

37. In this splendid view photographed from near Cogenhoe church on the beautiful spring morning of Sunday 8 April 1962, Ivatt tank No. 41219 works the 10.30 a.m. train from Wellingborough Midland Road to Northampton Castle along the Nene Valley. This pleasing scene over the gravel pits towards Northampton has changed dramatically through the years as the town has expanded its boundary, engulfing Little and Great Billing in the process. *(Tommy Tomalin courtesy Colour Rail)*

STEAM AROUND NORTHAMPTON TOWN

38. A rarely photographed location within Northampton was just east of Hardingstone Junction about a mile from Bridge Street station where the Northampton to Bedford line crossed the Northampton to Wellingborough route. During the last week of the Northampton to Bedford services at the beginning of March 1962, Standard tank No. 84005 sets off to Bedford with a morning train from Northampton. The sun has momentarily made an appearance to highlight the train. Of note is the Midland Railway distant signal standing proud as the train passes it. *(Brian Denny)*

39. The well loaded up Sunday diverted 'Ulster Express' works over 15 arches towards Roade and Euston on 4 March 1962 in the capable hands of Type 4 diesel No. D292 and Jubilee No. 45559 BRITISH COLUMBIA. Apparently the Jubilee was being used to heat the train, owing to heating problems with the boilers on the diesels, but if appearance is anything to go by, then the 'Jubilee' looks to be doing more than its fair share of the work as they pound up the 1 in 200 bank. *(Brian Denny)*

STEAM AROUND NORTHAMPTON TOWN

40. By travelling about 400 yards along the line to Wellingborough (in picture 38) one arrives at the lonely outpost of the Bedford Road crossing. Here the railway is at the end of a long 2 mile straight run from Billing, as shown in the picture above. For the road traveller on the A428 the crossing is on a severe bend when approached from Bedford. On the glorious summer evening of Monday 23 July 1962, Northampton Stanier class 5 No. 45051 heads towards Hardingstone Junction with the 6 p.m. Peterborough East to Northampton Castle local train where arrival time should be 7.29 p.m. after a 44 mile journey. 45051 spent a period of almost four years allocated to Northampton shed at this time. *(Tommy Tomalin)*

STEAM AROUND NORTHAMPTON TOWN

41. Stanier class 5 No. 45044 of Willesden shed passes Duston West signal-box with a London-bound meat train via Blisworth, on what was locally known, for obvious reasons, as 'bottom line', during the afternoon of Sunday 23 September 1962. The locomotive shed is visible in the distance under the bridge, actually in the triangle of lines based on Duston West, Duston North and Bridge Street Junctions. In the distant past an ironstone railway from Far Cotton to Duston Furnaces ran under the round-arched bridge to the right of the train parallel with the main line to Blisworth. The activity on 'top line' using what is believed to be the Rugby steam crane, is that of bridge deck renewal in connection with electrification, at that time three years away. In certain weather conditions the sound of a down express thundering over the old 'iron bridge' could be heard at Queen Eleanor Cross, a mile away. Needless to say, the concrete deck was never the same. The locomotive became a Northampton engine from February to August 1963. (*Graham Onley*)

42. A warm south-westerly breeze blows across the embankment by Duston West signalbox on Saturday 20 August 1960, as Nuneaton-based Hughes/Fowler 'Crab' class 2-6-0 No. 42939 slowly plods up the 1 in 200 gradient with a southbound ballast train. The engine will continue to climb through Hunsbury Hill tunnel and all the five miles to Roade station before the gradient slackens. This stretch of line from Castle station up to Hunsbury Hill proved very popular with both railway enthusiasts and photographers. (*Brian Denny*)

STEAM AROUND NORTHAMPTON TOWN

43. Fowler Patriot No. 45541 DUKE OF SUTHERLAND works smartly round the curve by Northampton sheds heading for Blisworth with a Rugby to Euston semi-fast that left Northampton Castle at 5.55 p.m. on this bright evening in April 1960. Four unrebuilt 'Patriots' were shedded at Rugby during this period, and it was not unusual to see one of these attractive locomotives on this train. In the background is Northampton's skyline – looking very industrial from this viewpoint. *(Brian Denny)*

44/45. The photographs on these two pages, taken on Thursday 17 May 1962, from Duston West signalbox, are an interesting comparison and show just how important the sun is to bring out the colours in colour photography. In the first photograph, taken around 6.30 p.m., the sun has almost disappeared as a diverted main line express pounds up the bank in the capable hands of Britannia class pacific No. 70042 LORD ROBERTS. Without the sun the colours take on a more sombre appearance and much detail is lost. In the second the sun is low but still bright as Wellingborough-based Standard 9F class 2-10-0 No. 92132 works steadily up the bank with a coal train bound for the south. The surroundings and town behind are bathed in sunlight illuminating much detail. In the background one of the Borough refuse destruction plant chimneys is being dismantled – another town landmark goes. *(both pictures Ron Gammage)*

STEAM AROUND NORTHAMPTON TOWN

46. The peace and tranquillity of a cold winter's evening at Duston West signalbox are disturbed by Stanier Mogul 2-6-0 No. 42953 on Wednesday 15 February 1961. Having backed off shed around 5 p.m., the locomotive catches the intense low light of the setting sun as she pulls forward, heading for Castle yards, to prepare her Manchester-bound freight train for a 7 p.m. departure time. This section of track now gives access to the Track Machine Training School at Briar Hill. *(Ron Gammage)*

47. At Rothersthorpe level crossing situated on the line between Northampton and Blisworth the diverted 'Royal Scot' hauled by Stanier Pacific No. 46250 CITY OF LICHFIELD is running well behind schedule as she eases over the crossing after a signal check. Unable to use the steam being produced by her boiler, owing to the slow progress, 46250's safety valves lift and steam roars into the evening atmosphere as the sun sinks to the horizon in this dramatic 1960s scene. *(Brian Denny)*

STEAM AROUND NORTHAMPTON TOWN

48. An unidentified rebuilt Royal Scot works a train of red and cream coaches over 15 arches viaduct as she heads for Roade and Euston via Hunsbury Hill tunnel in the summer of 1957. This is a seldom photographed view of 15 arches from the west side, with the River Nene winding its way through the main arch and giving a feeling of rural tranquillity which belies the fact that Northampton town centre is less than a mile away. *(Ron Gammage)*

49. The wild flowers on the wasteland, now part of Rothersthorpe Road Industrial Estate, make a very pleasing foreground as Fowler 4F class 0-6-0 No. 44219 from Northampton shed darkens the sky with clag being thrown from its chimney. The 4F is no doubt finding it a struggle to haul the heavily loaded freight up the 1 in 200 bank past Duston West signalbox on this lovely day in June 1960. 44219 was allocated to Northampton for an eight-year period from October 1954 to June 1962, and will be remembered by many local railwaymen. *(Brian Denny)*

STEAM AROUND NORTHAMPTON TOWN

50. Stanier Coronation Pacific No. 46239 CITY OF CHESTER, based at Willesden shed, coasts downhill past Duston West on Sunday 3 May 1964 at the head of a northbound parcels train. The possibility of a Coronation Pacific on this train had many a photographer up at the crack of dawn, and the combination of a bright spring morning and a relatively clean locomotive was ample reward. Until August 1963, 46239 had been a Camden allocated locomotive (since at least 1950) and, although a regular visitor to Northampton (but never on shed), it didn't seem to suffer the good natured verbal abuse aimed at many of our local staple diet of lesser locomotives. *(Graham Onley)*

51. Another view from Northampton No. 1 signalbox, this time on a very cold Sunday 23 March 1958, finds the diverted down 'Royal Scot' easing its way past Northampton Borough's West Bridge Depot. Having left the main line at Roade, the train will pass through platform 6 at Castle station before eventually regaining the main line at Rugby. The safety valves of Stanier Coronation Pacific No. 46237 CITY OF BRISTOL blow off vehemently as the steam pressure in the boiler exceeds the maxiumum 250 lbs per square inch allowable. 'City of Bristol' was one of the few in this class to have a red background to its nameplates. (Ross Smith)

52. Stanier Pacific No. 46238 CITY OF CARLISLE storms away from the south end of Hunsbury Hill tunnel on the rising gradient towards Roade with the up 'Carlisle' on a bitterly cold day in January 1960. En route the train has obviously encountered some snow which has stuck to the locomotive's buffers. A 'down' distant signal, that was situated on the south side of Hunsbury Hill tunnel and was controlled by Duston West signalbox, necessitated a mile-long pull right through the tunnel. This was motorized during the 1950s, thus making the signalman's life a little less strenuous. (Brian Denny)

53. Sunday 1 March 1959 was bright and clear, and once again the main line trains have been diverted through Northampton, this time taking the low level route via Blisworth. With steam to spare, Stanier's Jubilee class 4-6-0 No. 45738 SAMSON from Bushbury shed eases her way towards Northampton from Blisworth with a down Wolverhampton express. The farm track and footpath on the left was part of the track bed of the long gone Hunsbury Hill Ironstone Railway, an industrial line whose works and mines closed in 1921. *(Ron Gammage)*

54. On Tuesday 22 January 1963 a long empty coaching stock and parcels train heads for the West Coast main line having passed through Northampton. Hauled by Stanier Black 5 No. 44939, it storms through the winter landscape past Duston Sidings on the line to Blisworth at 2.05 p.m. A classic example of steam, snow and sun – a combination so often sought after by the railway photographer. *(Tommy Tomalin courtesy Colour Rail)*

55. On a typically dull and gloomy Sunday morning on 27 January 1963 in the severe winter of that year, a Stanier 8F No. 48609 of Kettering shed gives an effective response to the weather conditions by going all out up the bank out of Northampton at the start of the long climb to Roade, issuing steam and smoke in all directions, leaving it to condense profusely in the sub-zero atmosphere. Black with coal dust and white with water vapour, its discharged exhaust rises higher and to greater proportions than is normally seen. Another unusual aspect to this scene is that here is a freight working on a Sunday, hitherto not seen before by many on this route. The reason for this and other such Sunday freight workings during this winter spell was that such a backlog of unmoved goods had accumulated because of the severe conditions that any opportunity, such as an available spare locomotive and crew, had to be taken. *(Robin Puryer)*

Steam Around Northampton Town

56. The extreme cold of the winter of 1962/63 had already lasted for a month and railway services were still suffering. Coaching stock and freight vehicles were not in their correct places for the work schedules owing to the cancellation of trains and suspension of some services. On Saturday 26 January 1963 a long train works out of Northampton behind Black 5 No. 45328 from Warrington shed. Made up of assorted coaches, parcels vans, sleeping cars and other articulated stock, the Black 5 climbs very slowly past, taking the route south via Roade, with the locomotive and crew giving every indication they are in for a long hard struggle against the elements. *(Robin Puryer)*

57. On Tuesday 12 February 1963 the weather is starting to ease as a Stanier 8F heads off towards Market Harborough and the Nottingham coalfields with another rake of empty wagons. The signals at the junction of the lines to Rugby and Market Harborough stand like lonely sentinels watching the progress of the 8F through the snow-covered landscape. *(Tommy Tomalin)*

58. Saturday 3 November 1962 was bright and clear, with no hint of the severe winter to follow, as another Stanier 8F works in from Rugby past the branch to Market Harborough with an up mixed freight. Viewed from the stonewalled footpath beside Kingsthorpe village church, the shallow valley of the northern tributary of the River Nene gives way to the dense mass of trees belonging to Harlestone Firs on the horizon. *(Robin Puryer)*

59. The dreaded winter of 1963 is now well under way and breaking all kinds of records, with temperatures falling as low as 0°F(-18°C) overnight in Northamptonshire to 28°F(-2°C) in the daytime at best. Furthermore a clear blue sky was very unusual in this winter of gloom and dullness, thus making a very pleasant change on Saturday 19 January 1963. All over the country workmen were having to keep rails and trackside equipment clear with simple shovels as seen here at Mill Lane on the northern outskirts of Northampton where the snow had built up over the rails. Stanier Black 5 No. 44872 of Aston depot in Birmingham, not normally known for working to Northampton, has been given the job of working an unidentified Rugby to Euston all-stations local train working to an emergency timetable, and is seen here gliding almost silently towards Northampton. *(Robin Puryer)*

60. The fourth day of the coldest and longest period of snow this century, and the severe conditions have already affected railway services and caused train movements and locomotive scheduling to be rearranged. Here a Jubilee class 4-6-0, which would not normally have been allocated a slow freight duty, and certainly not a coal train, is seen running strongly despite the bitter cold with its heavy load as it blasts under Mill Lane bridge. The train is heading past Kings Heath on the connecting route to the Midland main line at Market Harborough at 2.10 p.m. on Saturday 29 December 1962 while the dull thick cloud promises more snow to come. Ironically the Jubilee No. 45626 was named SEYCHELLES after the warm tropical island in the Indian Ocean. *(Robin Puryer)*

Steam Around Northampton Town

61. Northampton Kingsthorpe Mill and the extremely cold winter of 1963 is well under way after ten days of snow and falling temperatures. Railway facilities are being impeded by the formation of solid ice and thus seizing up. Demand for extra coal for local power stations as well as for abnormally high levels of domestic use created the need for extra coal train movements and yet the weather is doing its best to prevent this. On Saturday 5 January Stanier '8F' 2-8-0 No. 48056 from Hasland shed, Chesterfield, is actually taking a short coal train in the opposite direction to normal from Northampton to Market Harborough. This was due apparently to an emergency transfer to alleviate a desperate shortage in Market Harborough. Not only was the locomotive an unusual visitor to Northampton but it was having to work in reverse – this was said to be because the turntable at Northampton shed was iced-up and inoperable. *(Robin Puryer)*

62. 12 January 1963, and the record-breaking winter continues, freezing day and night. The River Nene has frozen over and the Arctic wind has blown powdery snow over the ice so that the river cannot be distinguished. On the railway, Stanier 8F No. 48638 from Nottingham shed is seen charging out of Northampton, adjacent to Kingsthorpe Hollow, with a train of coal empties returning via Market Harborough and the Midland main line to the Nottinghamshire coalfields. In the background more oil tankers than usual have been brought in as the demand for heating fuel has grown. *(Robin Puryer)*

63. Although there were only ten converted Crosti-style Standard 2-10-0 locomotives, originally built with two boilers in an attempt (which failed) to improve the efficiency of even the most modern design of freight engine, it was not unusual to find one in or around Northampton, as they were allocated to Wellingborough or Kettering. However, it was not quite so easy to catch one of them working, but here is 92022 really going 'full steam ahead', crossing the River Nene between Kingsthorpe and Kings Heath with a long train of empty coal wagons bound for Nottingham on Saturday 3 November 1962. Northampton No. 5 signalbox in the background marks the junction where the Rugby and the Market Harborough lines meet. *(Robin Puryer)*

64. Saturday 1 December 1962 was a particularly foggy day, and as it was still thick at midday the fog seemed unlikely to clear, but well into the afternoon a low sun unexpectedly burst dramatically through the gloom, its strong yellow colour producing an effect the photographer had not seen before. He hastily rushed out from his home nearby and went for this master shot. Kettering-based Stanier 8F No. 48467 and its long train of empty coal wagons have been lit superbly as they pass No. 5 signalbox at Kings Heath, Northampton, and head in the direction of Market Harborough. *(Robin Puryer)*

STEAM AROUND NORTHAMPTON TOWN

Just over a mile north of Northampton No. 5 signalbox at Kingsthorpe Boughton crossing used to be the first signalbox on the Market Harborough branch where the line crossed the A50 road. On the evening of Wednesday 27 May 1964 two freight trains pass the box travelling in opposite directions within ten minutes of each other. The branch, which opened in 1858, had a staggered history in its final years. It was first closed to passengers on 4 January 1960 but reopened to through passenger traffic on 6 January 1969. With another closed spell between May 1969 and July 1972 the passenger service was finally withdrawn on 26 August 1973 and the line completely closed on 16 August 1981.

65/66. Stanier 8F 2-8-0 No. 48492 from Wellingborough brings a train of coal towards Northampton at 6.15 p.m. (left), while Standard 9F 2-10-0 No. 92049 works hard with a train to Nottingham at 6.25 p.m. (above). A large amount of freight traffic, especially coal and iron ore, travelled on this route even though some parts of the line were steeply graded and engines had to work hard. Kelmarsh tunnel with its narrow bore was particularly difficult for both engine and crew on the graded section. *(both pictures Tommy Tomalin)*

TO THE PREMIER LINE AND BEYOND

67/68. After arriving at Weedon from Southam with a rake of chalk empties, Standard 9F 2-10-0 No. 92103 has picked up further wagons from the siding ready for the trip southwards to Leighton Buzzard. In these two superb landscape views, taken around 4 p.m. on Sunday 1 October 1961, the 9F pulls out of the siding and heads away through Weedon station on the up main line. Situated on the right is the bay platform used for branch passenger traffic between Weedon and Leamington until cessation of services on 13 September 1958. *(both pictures Tommy Tomalin – 67 courtesy of Colour Rail)*

69. Stanier Jubilee class 4-6-0 No. 45741 LEINSTER roars up the 1 in 330 gradient through Althorp Park station, heading for Rugby with the 4.27 p.m. Euston to Wolverhampton express on Saturday 23 May 1959. *(Ross Smith)*

70 (below). A view of the exterior of Althorp Park station on the same day taken from the A428 Northampton to Rugby road. This was once the station for Althorp House and the scene in years gone by of many distinguished people arriving and departing. Alas the station was closed in 1960 and no trace of it remains. *(Ross Smith)*

71. A location half-a-mile east of Althorp Park station was the ideal spot chosen by the photographer to obtain an excellent side-on view of Britannia class No. 70020 MERCURY working a 9.15 a.m. special from Euston on Sunday 8 November 1964. The morning sunshine glints off the clean boiler of the locomotive as the exhaust sits above the train in the crisp cold air. At the time Willesden-based 70021 was rostered for several railtour duties and was kept in excellent condition. It ended its days in the Carlisle area and was finally withdrawn in January 1967. *(Tommy Tomalin courtesy of Colour Rail)*

TO THE PREMIER LINE AND BEYOND

72. It is the Saturday before Christmas, 23 December 1961, and rebuilt Royal Scot No. 46120 ROYAL INNISKILLING FUSILIER has arrived at Rugby Midland station with a special up parcels train. Close observation of the vans showed that they were marked for Maiden Lane in London, bringing some late Christmas mail from the north west of England. The locomotive is in reasonable external condition and perfectly positioned as the winter sun beats down on it while the cold northerly wind blows the exhaust from the chimney. *(Neville Simms)*

TO THE PREMIER LINE AND BEYOND

73. The down 'Shamrock' basks in the evening light adjacent to Rugby No.4 signalbox while awaiting the green flag to proceed northwards on 9 September 1961. The combination of the maroon Coronation class Pacific No. 46240 CITY OF COVENTRY hauling maroon coaches makes a very pleasing sight even though the locomotive was somewhat work stained. *(Neville Simms)*

74. The young lad looks on in amazement and thinks: 'Why are they putting water into a diesel, and where is the steam coming from?' At this time the trains were steam heated and the water was required for the train heating boiler. Normally this water would have been picked up via a scoop on the Newbold troughs, but on this particular Saturday, 23 December 1961, they were frozen. The Peak class 1Co-Co1 diesel No. D4 GREAT GABLE stands at the head on an 11 coach Carlisle to Euston train due out of Rugby at 2.30 p.m. *(Neville Simms)*

75. The brass nameplate of PRINCESS BEATRICE proudly stands out from her Brunswick green paintwork. *(Ross Smith)*

76. No longer used on the Anglo-Scottish and Liverpool expresses, but still looking every inch a lady, Princess Royal class Pacific No. 46209 PRINCESS BEATRICE stands patiently at Rugby Midland station with the 9.35 a.m. Wolverhampton to Euston express on Saturday 17 March 1962 amongst the usual gathering of spectators. *(Ross Smith)*

77. Amongst the general paraphernalia of Rugby station's platforms a driver looks on as the ticket inspector chats up two young ladies with their blonde bouffant hair styles who are patiently awaiting their train on Saturday 7 July 1962. Some things never change! *(Geoff Rixon)*

78. Time for a tea break for the engine crew at Rugby Midland station after the arrival of Coalville 4F class 0-6-0 No. 44501 from Leicester with a one-coach parcels train on Saturday 23 May 1964. Alas the engine, built by the North British Company in Glasgow in 1927 is a sad example of the run down state of many of the steam locomotives at this time as modernization was gradually phasing them out. *(Neville Simms)*

79. Late afternoon winter sunshine floods onto the platforms at Rugby Midland station on Saturday 2 February 1963 to coincide with the movement of Northampton Stanier class 5 No. 45050 shunting its empty coaching stock. 45050 and sister engine 45051 were used on regular passenger turns and became firm favourites with staff at the locoshed. 45050 remained allocated to Northampton until June 1964. *(Neville Simms)*

TO THE PREMIER LINE AND BEYOND

80. Annesley Standard 9F No. 92073 storms through Rugby Central with its Annesley to Woodford coal train on a freezing cold Saturday 21 December 1963. Frost was thick on the railway sleepers, even though it is midday, and the exhaust from the engine hangs motionless in the crisp winter air. This freight service was to prove to be the outstanding feature of the line in its last years. The 'windcutters', as the were called by the railwaymen, sped daily between Nottingham and Woodford as non-stop freights and became a showpiece of efficiency. What would BR have given to have the line in existence today with all the Channel Tunnel traffic! *(Neville Simms)*

81. Another fine example of a 9F in full flight through Rugby station with another freight bound for Woodford, once again on Saturday 21 December 1963. No. 92050 from Rowsley shed makes a superb winter spectacle even though the locomotive is in a poor external condition. All Great Central enthusiasts will mourn the loss of the Great Central railway, especially the sterling work of the 9F's during the final years of the line's existence. At least the excellent preservation work carried out at Loughborough will mean sights such as this will continue to be recreated on some part of the famous Great Central Railway. *(Neville Simms)*

TO THE PREMIER LINE AND BEYOND

82. On 25 May 1963, just two months after Charwelton station closed, the photographer managed to gain access to this unusual viewpoint from between the 4' 8 1/2" on the ironstone sidings as Stanier Jubilee class 4-6-0 No. 45561 SASKATCHEWAN works her way past Charwelton signalbox with a down parcels at 1.15 p.m. The up and down main lines are clearly indicated by the soot marks on the bridge during this very pleasant afternoon. (*Tommy Tomalin*)

TO THE PREMIER LINE AND BEYOND

83. Banbury-based Hall class 4-6-0 No. 6911 HOLKER HALL speeds the Bournemouth to Sheffield Victoria holiday train through Woodford Halse and past the carriage and wagon repair depot on Saturday 15 July 1961. The engine and crew would work as far as Leicester and then return to Banbury on another southbound train. Woodford No.2 signalbox stands on the right. Sometimes called 'North Loop' it was Woodford's busiest box, controlling movements to and from the up and down sidings and from the sheds and wagon shop. *(Brian Denny)*

It's Cup Final day on Saturday 25 May 1963 between Leicester City and Manchester United, resulting in a number of trains running via the Great Central between Leicester Central and Wembley Hill for the match which Manchester United won 3-1, thus ensuring Leicester were losing finalists in the FA Cup twice in three years.

84. An excellent viewpoint was obtained here at Charwelton troughs by climbing the ladder of the down distant signal. As other enthusiasts gather by the water tank supplying the troughs one of Burton shed's spotless Jubilees No. 45598 BASUTOLAND picks up water as she sweeps southwards at 12.32 p.m. with an all 1st class special. *(Tommy Tomalin courtesy Colour Rail)*

85. Another spit-and-polished Jubilee from Burton shed No. 45626 SEYCHELLES roars past with another special for Wembley as her driver opens the regulator after leaving the confines of Catesby tunnel at the summit of the 6-mile climb from Braunston. Photographically the area around Charwelton proved very rewarding for local enthusiasts with many excellent locations and a gradient approaching the station from both directions, making sure engines were working hard. *(John Harrison)*

TO THE PREMIER LINE AND BEYOND

86. The photographer and some friends were out for a local train ride and shed bash on Sunday 9 September 1962. After travelling to Rugby Midland they transferred to Rugby Central station with the intention of visiting Woodford Halse and Banbury sheds. The train to Woodford Halse was hauled by B1 class 4-6-0 No. 61039 STEINBOK, but on alighting and visiting the shed they were refused entry by a sarcastic foreman who retorted: 'I've got better things to do than walking around with a sack picking up severed arms and legs.' After trudging back to the station Sid Bellham captured this pleasing shot of Black 5 4-6-0 No. 44821 before their train arrived to take the party to Banbury where their shed visit was more successful. The day was topped by a fantastic run over Staverton bank behind Sheffield Darnall B1 class 4-6-0 No. 61051 on the way back to Rugby. *(Sid Bellham)*

87. An 'Annesley Runner' or 'Windcutter' emerges from Catesby tunnel behind Standard 9F class 2-10-0 No. 92095 as it nears journey's end at Woodford Halse on 25 May 1963. This freight service, which ran mostly loose coupled, had been launched in 1947 and was the epitome of efficient working. It ran on an 'out and back' principle with the time taken to wait for the return working from Woodford being kept to a minimum. When it finished in June 1965 it sealed the fate of the Great Central Railway which closed a year later. *(John Harrison)*

TO THE PREMIER LINE AND BEYOND

88. Having just passed Brackley Central station, Bullied West Country class Pacific No. 34002 SALISBURY heads north with an RCTS Great Central railtour on Saturday 13 August 1966. The train was travelling very fast with 'Salisbury' working on full regulator, and prior to it coming into view the photographer thought the train was being diesel hauled, such was the sound of the exhaust. Complete with Southern Region coaching stock, the tour began at Waterloo and travelled via Neasden, Harrow and the Great Central to Nottingham Victoria, Mansfield, Rotherham, Sheffield, back to Nottingham Victoria and down to High Wycombe, terminating at Marylebone. Apart from 'Salisbury', a Stanier 8F, Thompson B1 and an Electric Locomotive were used on the round trip. *(Tony Pirie)*

89. The Great Western Railway main line sweeps through Northampton-shire in the south-west corner of the county. In this photograph, taken at Kings Sutton, '5100' class 2-6-2T No. 4151 of Leamington shed heads north with an afternoon limestone train on a particularly beautiful summer Saturday, 4 July 1964. The limestone originated at Ardley Quarry and is bound for the cement works adjacent to Greaves sidings near Harbury, a journey of some 24 miles. *(David Pick)*

TO THE PREMIER LINE AND BEYOND

90. Although water troughs were a familiar feature in the steam days there were only two locations in Northamptonshire where they could be seen. One was in the south-western tip of the county on the Great Western main line at Aynho and the other on the Great Central at Charwelton, near Woodford, also on the west side of the county. In this illustration Castle class 4-6-0 No. 5033 BROUGHTON CASTLE takes water as it storms through Aynho troughs with a summer Saturday train from Bournemouth West to Manchester/Liverpool on 23 June 1962. Black smoke pours out of the engine's chimney as water can be seen cascading at the back of the tender. The River Cherwell on the right hand side forms the county boundary with Oxfordshire on the other side. Sadly Broughton Castle, an Oxford-based engine, was to be withdrawn from traffic within two months. *(Neville Simms)*

TO THE PREMIER LINE AND BEYOND

91. Holbrook Park water troughs, a couple of miles west of Rugby on the line to Coventry, is the scene on a dismal summer Saturday 30 June 1962. Rebuilt Royal Scot No. 46147 THE NORTHAMPTONSHIRE REGIMENT, based at Willesden shed in London, takes water as it speeds towards Wolverhampton with the 8.45 a.m. train from Euston via Northampton where it departed at 10.19 a.m. after a three minute stop. Sadly 46147 was withdrawn within six months, after 35 years in service. *(Neville Simms)*

92. A winter's day at Banbury station as Hall class 4-6-0 No. 6923 CROXTETH HALL stands in the bay platform with a train for Woodford Halse. The misty murky conditions are dull enough to make the lamp on the front of the locomotive shine bright as a member of the footplate crew walks up the platform ready for his next duty armed with his traditional billy-can of tea. It is Saturday 4 January 1964 and the Oxford-based locomotive will remain in service for two more years before withdrawal. *(David Pick)*

93. Banbury station on Thursday 24 May 1962 resembles a scene that is still very similar today. Rebuilt Royal Scot class No. 46118 ROYAL WELCH FUSILIER stands in the bay platform with an afternoon train to Woodford Halse, normally a duty for a Woodford 2-6-4 tank engine. On the adjacent platform Hall class No. 6906 CHICHELEY HALL, a locally based engine, waits with a parcels van. Remarkably, steam-hauled special trains still stop at the station today to enable the locomotive to take water while en route between Didcot and Stratford-upon-Avon or Sheffield. The special trains normally run at weekends, and many folk still come to see the steam locomotives. Let us hope this continues for many years to come. (Ken Fairey)

TO THE PREMIER LINE AND BEYOND

94. A hot summer Saturday at the south end of Banbury station finds Castle class 4-6-0 No. 5089 WESTMINSTER ABBEY busy shunting wagons before heading south on 15 June 1963. 5089 started life as 'Star' class No. 4069 before being rebuilt as a 'Castle' engine and renumbered in 1939. By now all the 'Castles' had finished on the Paddington-Birmingham passenger services and were used on more mundane duties. The engine was based at Stafford Road for just a few more months before becoming an Oxley engine. It was finally withdrawn in November 1964. *(Robin Puryer)*

TO THE PREMIER LINE AND BEYOND

95. A splendid scene at the south end of Banbury station on the evening of Thursday 26 April 1962. This was a favourite location for many train-spotters and photographers in the area. Not only the main line passenger and freight trains but all the activity in and out of Banbury locomotive shed could be observed. As a number of railwaymen and workers head for the station the gathering of train-spotters peer across the tracks as Castle class No. 5002 LUDLOW CASTLE, a Swindon-based locomotive, eases past with a northbound empty coaching stock train. (Ken Fairey)

96. A gloomy cold Saturday 4 January 1964 at Banbury shed shows another Banbury favourite Modified Hall class 4-6-0 No. 7912 LITTLE LINFORD HALL simmering in between duties. The locomotive arrived at Banbury in April 1962 and remained at the shed until withdrawal in October 1965. Whenever weather conditions were dull, the atmosphere thickened at any steam shed; steam and smoke mingling with the cold damp air, creating that never-to-be-forgotten sulphurous smell only found at a locoshed. *(David Pick)*

TO THE PREMIER LINE AND BEYOND

97. A Sunday afternoon visit to Banbury shed on 8 March 1964 shows a long-surviving Banbury engine Hall class No. 6906 CHICHELEY HALL basking in the springtime sunshine with Grange class No. 6825 LLANVAIR GRANGE alongside. About 30 other locomotives were present on this occasion. Alas 6906 was only to survive another 12 months before withdrawal. Banbury shed became LMR property in September 1963 and was allocated the shed code 2D compared to its Great Western code of 84C. After 56 years in existence it closed in October 1966, and the 12 remaining engines were transferred to no fewer than eight other London Midland sheds. *(David Pick)*

98. At 9.55 a.m. on the lovely morning of 12 October 1963 a Northampton to Woodford West freight works purposefully up the 1 in 171 gradient between Blisworth and Tiffield on the Stratford-upon-Avon and Midland Junction Railway in the capable hands of Stanier Black 5 class 4-6-0 No. 45287. The train is about to pass Blisworth ironstone sidings and is a view so typical of the rural tranquillity of this cross-country branch line. At the time Stanier Black 5s from Northampton shed were regularly used on this trip, but a few years earlier smaller 0-6-0 locomotives of class 3F and 4F worked all the services over this section of the S.M.J.R., and struggled with their loads on odd occasions. *(Tommy Tomalin)*

TO THE PREMIER LINE AND BEYOND

99. Everything is quiet and peaceful at Blisworth as the shadows lengthen on the cold and clear Sunday of 9 December 1962, as indeed it had been all day for the trains were being diverted via Northampton owing to emergency works on the main line. Even so, this pleasing scene was so typical of Blisworth, and one seen many times over the years by railway enthusiasts young and old as they glanced back towards the station whilst making their way to the fields adjacent to Gayton Loops. Today's view bears no resemblance. With the S.M.J.R., sidings and loops all lifted, the new A43 dual carriageway cuts across the scene, with the road embankment and bridges situated between the S.M.J.R. signalbox and the station. *(Robin Puryer)*

100. The summer of 1956 finds Britannia class Pacific No. 70032 TENNYSON coasting northwards from Blisworth station with steam to spare hauling a down express made up entirely of red and cream coaching stock. In the sidings empty chalk wagons await return to Leighton Buzzard, while beyond piles of timber are stacked for 'seasoning', before the days of mass 'kiln drying'. A glance at the locomotive indicates that cleanliness was a thing of the past, even in 1956. *(John Harrison)*

TO THE PREMIER LINE AND BEYOND

101. Another summer 1956 photograph at Gayton signalbox captures Stanier Black 5 class 4-6-0 No. 45299 powering by the track works with an express freight bound for Carlisle. The definition 'express freight' meant that the train must be pipe-fitted throughout, with the automatic vacuum brake operative on a percentage of the goods truck; in this case 50 per cent. *(John Harrison)*

102. The photographer was always on the lookout for a good viewpoint, and this superb panorama at Blisworth was obtained by climbing onto the water tower at the south end of the station on the overcast day of 3 February 1962. It is 11.30 a.m. and an up express hurtles towards Euston past Kettering's Stanier 8F class 2-8-0 No. 48107, whose safety valves roar impatiently while awaiting access onto the main line, with a freight train that reaches right round the curve towards Northampton. On the left, wagons of iron ore stand on the ex-Stratford-upon-Avon and Midland Junction Railway sidings, as another 8F busies itself on shunting duties. *(Tommy Tomalin)*

103. On the same day, from the road bridge north of Blisworth station the time is 9 a.m. and the fireman of Northampton Stanier 8F class 2-8-0 No. 48440 has picked up the single line token from the signalman in the S.M.J. signalbox. After rejoining the footplate the driver opens up the 8F for a run at the 1 in 171 bank that was on a sharp curve as the single line meandered its way through the countryside towards Towcester and Stratford-upon-Avon. *(Tommy Tomalin)*

TO THE PREMIER LINE AND BEYOND

104. Many train-spotters local to Northampton will remember 'the shed' over the Northampton branch bay at Blisworth, as indeed they will remember Ivatt class 2-6-2 tank No. 41218, seen here taking in the sunshine on the Blisworth motor set during Sunday 29 October 1961. This train left Northampton at 12.03 p.m. to connect with up and down expresses on the West Coast main line, and is seen waiting patiently for them to arrive. 41218 was allocated new to Northampton in 1948 and remained a local resident until withdrawal in 1965. *(Tommy Tomalin)*

105. Stanier Duchess class Pacific No. 46247 CITY OF LIVERPOOL was one of the first Duchesses to be repainted in red livery during May 1958, and is seen still in pristine condition as she races through the Northamptonshire countryside past Gayton loops with the down 'Ulster Express' on Sunday 15 June 1958. *(Ron Gammage)*

To the Premier Line and Beyond

106. While the photographer was cycling from his previous campsite at Gayton Loops to a new campsite in Roade Cutting on Tuesday 25 August 1964, he was lucky enough to catch this shot of Stanier Pacific No. 46256 SIR WILLIAM A. STANIER, F.R.S. hurrying across the bridge over the A43 with the up 'Lakes Express'. The yellow stripe on the cabside meant that these locomotives were not for use under the wires south of Crewe after 1 September. Some local train-spotters did not know this at the time and thought BR was carrying out some kind of experiment on the locomotives, but once the stripe's purpose became common knowledge realization finally set in that life would never be the same again. Amazingly, considering the local annual holiday period is in full swing, the A43 is deserted. Also of note is the road sign which is rather misleading, as sadly by this time Blisworth station no longer existed. *(Graham Onley)*

107. Northampton Stanier 8F class 2-8-0 No. 48754 is really getting back to nature as she gingerly makes for Ravenstone Wood Junction, 1¼ miles away, while hauling the track lifting train at 11.10 a.m. on Sunday 6 September 1964. This was the section of the Stratford-upon-Avon and Midland Junction Railway line that connected Towcester with Olney and Bedford. Apart from the odd excursion between the Midland Division and Stratford, the branch was used solely for freight movements until its closure on 30 June 1958. A local passenger service was tried out from 1 December 1892 but ceased after only four months because of lack of use. *(Tommy Tomalin)*

TO THE PREMIER LINE AND BEYOND

Photographic views from Roade Junction signalbox are particularly rare, but we are pleased to show a series of colour pictures taken by the late local RCTS member Keith Locke, who regularly visited the signalbox in the last years of steam. To stand on the platform at Roade station and hear and see the steam trains speeding through will long be a memory for the many train-spotters who were there, yet to have been in the signalbox must have been even more exciting.

108. Rebuilt Patriot class No. 45531 SIR FREDERICK HARRISON tears through with an up express from Liverpool to Kensington Olympia on the afternoon of Saturday 19 October 1963. *(Keith Locke)*

109 (below). Rugby-shedded Stanier class 5 No. 45044 crosses from fast to slow lines with the 2.40 p.m. Blisworth to Reading parcels train on Saturday 27 July 1963. *(Keith Locke)*

110. In glorious evening sunlight Princess Royal Pacific No. 46208 PRINCESS HELENA VICTORIA eases the down 'Merseyside Express' past Roade Junction signalbox after a signal check on 2 July 1960. An exciting feature of the Merseyside Express's departure from Euston at 6.05 p.m. was the race that ensued on most evenings with the 6.06 p.m. from Euston to Northampton. The latter, usually headed by a class 5 and running on the slow lines, generally overhauled the much heavier Liverpool express before Willesden, and sometimes even reached its first stop at Kings Langley before the 'Merseyside Express' swept majestically past. *(Sid Bellham)*

TO THE PREMIER LINE AND BEYOND

By the middle of 1963 many BR Standard Britannia class locomotives were being used between London and Birmingham and beyond on both passenger and freight traffic. Summer Saturday trains were no exception, and here are three of Willesden's examples at Roade Junction. The 'Brits' proved to be the most successful of all Riddle's standard designs and certainly in the Northampton area the well-proportioned lines of these Pacifics became popular with many enthusiasts.

111. 70034 THOMAS HARDY accelerates through Roade station with the 10 a.m. Llandudno to Euston express on 27 July 1963. Allocated to Longsight Manchester when new in December 1952, this example had always worked on the L.M.R. Note the green coloured nameplate compared to the red of the other two examples illustrated. *(Keith Locke)*

TO THE PREMIER LINE AND BEYOND

112 (above). 70014 IRON DUKE passes with the 2.45 p.m. Euston to Northampton train, also on 27 July 1963. This engine started life by working on boat trains from London to Dover in 1951, including the famous 'Golden Arrow'. *(Keith Locke)*

113. 70012 JOHN OF GAUNT is surprisingly crossed from fast to slow hauling the 10 a.m. Llandudno to Euston on 10 August 1963. This example was first allocated to the Great Eastern at Norwich in May 1951 to work express passenger services to Liverpool Street, London. *(Keith Locke)*

114. There was seldom a more stirring sight in steam days than a Duchess on full regulator, as this photograph shows. Photographed at Ashton, Pacific No. 46221 QUEEN ELIZABETH storms towards Euston with a well-loaded express from Carlisle. The fireman must be feeding coal into the firebox judging by the pall of smoke emanating from the chimney on this dull and overcast Thursday 12 April 1962. 46221 was fitted with a streamlined casing when built in 1937 and had the distinction of carrying all three streamlined liveries consisting of blue with white stripes from new, red with gold stripes from March 1941 and black from October 1944 until the casing was removed in May 1946. 'Queen Elizabeth' is seen here in the Standard British Railways green livery. (Ken Fairey)

115. Just over two weeks later at Ashton on Tuesday 24 April 1962 the weather has changed for the better as the sun highlights the all red livery combination on the down 'Shamrock', sweeping northwards through the cold evening air behind Stanier's Duchess Pacific No. 46229 DUCHESS OF HAMILTON. Fortunately, with 46229 being in preservation, sights similar to this can be seen out on the main line even today, although not in quite such a workaday condition. 46229 was also streamlined when new in 1938, being painted in red and gold striped livery, and in 1939 was temporarily disguised as No. 6220 with CORONATION nameplates for a visit across the Atlantic to tour America. It covered 3,121 miles before being placed on exhibition at the New York World Fair. On returning to England the locomotive reverted to its original identity. *(Ken Fairey)*

TO THE PREMIER LINE AND BEYOND

TO THE MIDLAND LINE AND BEYOND

116. Station approach to Kettering station on Friday 4 October 1963 shows a scene that is still remarkably similar today, at least as far as the station building is concerned. It is unlikely one would now see such a collection of cars of the period. The official entrance to the locoshed is on the right but in those days train-spotters could get a sneaky entrance to the back end (well, as far as their courage let them) by creeping down the alley between the rear of the station refreshment room and the shed and past the bike sheds. Those were the days!. *(Roger West)*

117. A pleasant evening at Kettering shed with the ever-present Standard 9Fs in residence. No. 92122 from Leicester shed and No. 92106, one of Kettering's own 9Fs, stand simmering ready for their next duty on Friday 1 May 1964. As the shadows lengthen a driver sets off homeward with his billy-can swinging in his hand. The sunlight on the shed picks out the ornamental brickwork and arched openings. The shed was built in 1876 by local Kettering builder C.Deakin for the grand sum of £7,488. It remained in operation for almost 90 years before being closed on 13 June 1965, and was later demolished. Alas, the space has been sacrificed to appease the automobile god as it now acts as the station car park. *(Roger West)*

TO THE MIDLAND LINE AND BEYOND

118/119. A look at Kettering station on Saturday 2 May 1964 shows a typical view of local trains in the platforms. Stanier class 5 No. 45270, wearing the 1H Northampton shed plate, arrives in platform 5 with the 2.05 p.m. Northampton to Leicester train. The distinctive Midland Railway platform canopies are well in evidence on both platforms 4 and 5. Once arrived, a handful of passengers board the train whilst a couple of railwaymen with bag and enamel billy-can head for the coach, probably seeking 'the cushions' for a journey north. Thanks are due to members of Kettering Civic Society who prevailed upon BR to retain the canopy and its ironwork, so that today one can still admire the superb Victorian workmanship. 45270 left Northampton shed the following month after only a six month stay. *(both pictures Roger West)*

120. Crossing the platforms by the underpass brings one to bay platform 1 which in earlier days was used for the Cambridge services. Ivatt 2MT class No. 41225 stands with the Northampton motor train on the last day of service. The platform is cluttered with parcels, cardboard for despatch and station trolleys so typical of this era. More parcels are being unloaded whilst dad takes his children for a wander along the platform. *(Roger West)*

TO THE MIDLAND LINE AND BEYOND

121. Monday 6 May 1963 finds Fowler 2-6-4 tank No. 42338 moving onto Kettering locoshed at around 7 p.m. after hauling the 5.57 p.m. local train down from Leicester. Although its duties are over for an hour, the safety valves lift, sending the rooks soaring and squawking into the sky on this very pleasant evening. Preservation crew members should note, not all footplatemen wore the grease top – a flat cap sufficed for many. The Fowler 2-6-4 tanks were handsome locomotives, although they were seemingly an ill thought of design. *(Roger West)*

TO THE MIDLAND LINE AND BEYOND

122. This quite remarkable panoramic view of the shed yard at Kettering, looking north, shows as many as a dozen locomotives in steam ready for the next day's activities on the dull Sunday afternoon of 5 April 1964. Already the gas lamps are lit, showing how overcast conditions really were, but the opportunity given to the photographer by a local fireman to gain access to the 80ft high water softening tower was too good to miss whatever the weather. After nearly 30 years perhaps the fireman can have a wry smile that his invitation led to this picture. *(Roger West)*

123. At Kettering shed on Saturday 13 March 1965 Leicester's visiting Standard class 2 No. 78027 is coaled up ready for the return journey. Coaling up was a filthy job, and the small steel skips had to be skidded across the steel-plated floor by hand to the tipping position. The coaling plant itself was a typical Midland Railway structure built in the 1870s. The openings were filled in with corrugated sheets during World War II to prevent light emission during the blackout. *(Roger West)*

124. A superb landscape view across the Welland Valley from south of Gretton on Sunday 6 November 1965 finds Stanier 8F No. 48317 toiling up the gradient towards Corby tunnel with a heavily loaded coal train. On reaching the tunnel, the gradient still rises and the hard-working locomotive will quickly fill the bore with smoke, making conditions very unpleasant for the 8F's footplate crew, especially as the tunnel exceeds a mile in length. *(Tommy Tomalin)*

TO THE MIDLAND LINE AND BEYOND

125. Saturday morning 4 August 1962 was bright and sunny at Glendon South Junction as children on the far bank witness the passage of Wellingborough 8F No. 48385 clanking past from Corby with a rake of empty wagons. Some freights would stop here, and the loco run round its train before proceeding northwards to Leicester, but not this one as there isn't a guard's van next to the engine. In the distance Glendon North Junction signalbox on the Leicester line is just visible under the smoke. Both the sides of the cutting and land in the background are spoil banks from old ironstone workings. Of all that is in view, only the triangle of stone at the very tip of the junction is virgin ground. (Roger West)

126. On Saturday morning 25 May 1963 Kettering 8F No. 48180 shunts Desborough goods yard picking up 'smalls traffic' generated from Desborough and Rothwell shoe factories. The covered semi-trailers parked under the goods shed canopy are successors to the Midland Railway's Thorneycroft steam wagons which operated from Desborough just after the turn of the century. *(Roger West)*

TO THE MIDLAND LINE AND BEYOND

127. Having worked out to Desborough from Kettering on Saturday morning 24 March 1965, double-chimneyed 9F No. 92231 comes to rest as the fireman climbs down to uncouple the train. This done the 9F will pull forward across the points, then back into the siding behind the wagon to pick up loaded ore wagons from Desborough quarries. The buildings on the bank acted as stables for the horses that used to haul wagons at the nearby quarries before the company owned their own steam locomotives. *(Roger West)*

128. Running easily after breasting Desborough summit, with the water tower in the background, Standard 9F No. 92117 drifts through Desborough and Rothwell station and the few miles towards Glendon Junction with a train of tube empties on Saturday morning 25 May 1963. On reaching Glendon Junction the 9F will stop and run round its train. The guard's van behind the tender will then become the rear of the train for the remaining half dozen miles to Corby. Neat and tidy gardens on Desborough and Rothwell station abound with flowers, and the splitting distant signal looks exceptionally smart having recently been repainted. *(Roger West)*

129. A wander down Merry Tom Lane, off the A50 road about a mile north of Chapel Brampton, brings one down to the Northampton to Market Harborough line. Here the lane crossed the line and continued to Brixworth. An occupation bridge just north of the crossing is the vantage point for a photograph of a typical freight train of the period as Standard 9F No. 92070 travels north on another superb evening on Wednesday 9 May 1962. In the distant background Pitsford and Brampton station is located, although this closed in 1950. With the fine efforts of the dedicated volunteers of the Northampton-Lamport Railway Group trains will again run on this stretch of line, recreating the good old days. *(Tommy Tomalin)*

130. Kelmarsh station was situated some five miles south of Market Harborough on the branch to Northampton. Although the station closed in January 1960 the signalbox remained open as many steam (and later diesel) hauled freight trains still used this useful route from north to south. On Saturday morning 12 September 1964 the photographer has chosen another fine day to use his camera. A 9F class 2-10-0 No. 92078 from Toton shed, in terrible external condition, works past the signalbox with a southbound empty ironstone train at 9.45 a.m.. *(Tommy Tomalin courtesy Colour Rail)*

TO THE MIDLAND LINE AND BEYOND

131. A peaceful scene at Market Harborough shed on Saturday 4 May 1963 as the locomotives stand simmering after their Saturday morning labours. Local 8F class No. 48467 keeps company with Colwick WD 2-8-0 'Austerity' class No. 90259, both locomotives looking well work-stained. The next time they will be disturbed will be during Sunday afternoon when the firelighter begins his job. Then the silence will be broken by this unseen worker as fire irons clang against the firebox. Later acrid fumes will appear to remind local residents that the short break from working steam locomotives will have ended. Although not recognisable in this illustration, the water tank at the shed was an integral part of the shed roof. The shed finally closed on 4 October 1965. *(Roger West)*

To the Midland Line and Beyond

132. A typical railway scene from the north end of Market Harborough station shows Wellingborough-based Fowler 4F 0-6-0 No. 44203 performing shunting duties on Monday morning 25 May 1964. In the background another similarly dirty 4F stands near the shed overlooked by the houses in Great Bowden Road. Market Harborough No.2 signalbox stands to the right controlling movements in and out of this part of the station area. *(Roger West)*

133. Saturday 18 November 1961 was one of those November days when the sun shone all day and made colour railway photography extremely rewarding. At the north end of Peterborough North station locally shedded Thompson A2/3 class Pacific No. 60500 EDWARD THOMPSON marshalls a train to form the next service to Kings Cross during the afternoon. The North Box signalbox stands proud, overlooking the shunting manoeuvres. The New England locomotive is in excellent external condition and shows the new BR emblem on the tender. 60500 was designed by Thompson in May 1946 and emerged as an 'A2' class locomotive, but when Thompson retired in 1947 it became an 'A2/3' class example of which there were 15 built altogether. *(Brian Denny)*

134. The north end of Peterborough North station on Saturday 25 August 1962 sees A3 class Pacific No. 60105 VICTOR WILD waiting for departure with the 1 p.m. Kings Cross to Edinburgh express due to leave at 2.32 p.m. The driver seems somewhat concerned with the underside of his engine. A regular watering stop for locomotives, Peterborough North was the station to observe the many L.N.E.R. Pacifics close at hand, and plenty of local train-spotters could be found on the platforms during the steam days, especially on summer Saturdays. *(Neville Simms)*

TO THE MIDLAND LINE AND BEYOND

135/136. On Saturday 16 November 1963 the photographer caught a train to Peterborough East with the intention of visiting New England locomotive shed on the Great Northern main line, but he surely could not have foreseen the exceptional lighting conditions that the late afternoon sun was to provide, although Sid Bellham did seem to have a knack of being in the right place at the right time in this respect. The setting winter sun's low light gave the locomotives a golden hue, and even the five grubby run-down A4s that were in store took on a new light, as the photograph of No. 60032 GANNET shows. Another view at the running shed (next page) finds the sun highlighting Peppercorn class A1 Pacific No. 60158 ABERDONIAN brewing up ready for its next turn of duty. Having 'bunked' the shed, he was on the point of leaving when he was challenged and sent packing by a burly Transport Policeman sporting a military moustache. *(both pictures Sid Bellham)*

To the Midland Line and Beyond

To the Midland Line and Beyond

137/138. On the same day that pictures 135 and 136 were taken, Saturday 16 November 1963, the photographer had experienced a most enjoyable train ride along the Nene Valley behind Fairburn 2-6-4 tank No. 42114 on the 9.13 a.m. from Northampton Castle, which arrived at Peterborough East around 10.45 a.m. This left just enough time to locate a position for photographing the 10.55 a.m. Saturdays-only train departing for Leicester. The exceptional lighting conditions prevailed even at this time of the morning, as we see the Hughes Fowler 'Crab' 2-6-0 No. 42896 of Nottingham shed pull the train out of the station and head vigorously past the signalbox towards Leicester. The photographer returned to Northampton in the evening well-satisfied with his visit to Peterborough's two stations, as well as the unauthorised trip around New England shed. *(both pictures Sid Bellham)*

139. On Sunday 4 October 1964 the photographer travelled to Peterborough to photograph a 'Home Counties Railway Society' special, expecting the train to be hauled by one of Stanier's Coronation Pacifics as advertised in previous publicity. Unfortunately, the remaining Coronation Pacifics in service had all been withdrawn the previous week, so the train was worked by Britannia Pacific No. 70020 MERCURY, a regular performer on specials around this time, and kept in commendable condition for the purpose by the cleaners at Willesden shed. Having left Kings Cross at 9.15 a.m., we see 'Mercury' and its train passing under the road bridge at Peterborough North, easing for the speed restriction through the station, as it heads towards its York destination. The morning sun had broken through the mist just at the right time, providing very good lighting conditions, and the photographer went home well pleased. The cost of this round trip to York from Kings Cross was just 55s (£2.75). *(David Pick)*

140. Christmas Eve 1962 was brilliantly clear and cloudless all day in our part of the country, but it was bitterly cold with a strong freezing wind. From the yard south of the station at Sandy, the nearest point on the Great Northern main line from Kings Cross for the railway photographers of Northampton, a rather grimy ex-L.N.E.R. class V2 No. 60982 slips a little as its large driving wheels try to grip the icy rails, its clear exhaust condensing quickly in the sharp cold air and catching the last rays of the setting sun. The 2-6-0 is restarting a rather long train of miscellaneous vans, heading for its home depot of York at about 3 p.m. Even though the sun is still shining, frost from the previous night is still visible on the wooden sleepers. *(Robin Puryer)*

TO THE MIDLAND LINE AND BEYOND

141. The 5 p.m. all stations Cambridge to Kettering train (Kettering arrive 6.38 p.m.) passes Raunds signalbox behind Ivatt class 2 No. 46404 on Monday 11 May 1959. The Midland style signalbox was normally 'switched out', being only used for control of entry into the goods yard. Amongst the railway enthusiasts who attended Raunds County Modern School was a group from Ringstead. Their station at Ringstead was situated on the Northampton to Peterborough line where larger and more modern locomotives were to be seen, in complete contrast to the veteran Great Eastern locomotives of the JI5 class that frequented Raunds station. The Ringstead boys, who were fiercely partisan towards their locomotives, would taunt the Raunds contingent about the old locomotives at Raunds and ensuing arguments regularly resulted in a free-for-all. *(Ian L. Wright)*

142. The 2.10 p.m. from Kettering to Cambridge calls at the tiny platform at Grafham on Saturday 30 May 1959 with Kettering's Ivatt class 2 No. 46496 in charge. The signalbox controlled level crossing gates over the country road from Ellington to Perry and Staughton. No. 46496 had the dubious honour of hauling the last passenger train on the line from Huntingdon to Kettering. *(Ian L. Wright)*

143. The last passenger trains on the Kettering-Huntingdon line ran on Saturday 13 June 1959, and during the last week teacher Ian Wright took 120 Raunds school children on trips from Raunds station to Kimbolton and back. The children of this small rural school only rarely encountered trains, and a few had reached the age of 11 without having travelled on one. On Wednesday 10 June 1959 the Raunds school children are on the platform at Kimbolton as class 2 No. 46496 arrives with the 5.00 p.m. Cambridge to Kettering which will take them back to Raunds. The group had arrived by the train on the left which is the 5.25 p.m. from Kettering hauled by No. 46467. The fare for this ride into history was 9d return. *(Ian L. Wright)*

TO THE MIDLAND LINE AND BEYOND

144. There were three trains each way on the Kettering-Cambridge line with no Sunday Service. This is the evening train to Cambridge – the 5.25 p.m. ex-Kettering standing at Raunds station on Tuesday 9 June 1959, consisting of two Eastern Region Gresley coaches and a horse box for Newmarket behind class 2 locomotive No. 46467. This train crossed the Kettering-bound train at Kimbolton where the respective locomotives exchanged crews. The platform oil lamp and signalbox opposite the goods shed convey the Midland Railway atmosphere of this branch line although the nameboard has a background of Eastern Region blue. *(Ian L. Wright)*

145. An Ivatt class 2 2-6-0 runs non-stop through Raunds station with the 7.35 a.m. train from Cambridge on Wednesday 3 June 1959. Raunds station was very poorly patronized. Its infrequent train service and 1½ mile walk from the town attracted few passengers. The passenger services ceased less than two weeks later, but goods trains (Kettering-Kimbolton) continued to serve Raunds until 28 October 1963. The photographer, a teacher at Raunds County Modern School, reminiscing about the Kettering to Cambridge line, summed it up as follows: 'The line held a special appeal for me; occasionally during the summer months I used to go to Raunds station during school lunchtimes, and enjoy the peace and beauty of the setting, with the singing of the birds in the bushes and the larks overhead being the only sounds on this rural cross-country branch line.' *(Ian L. Wright)*

TO THE MIDLAND LINE AND BEYOND

146. Long after the passenger services ceased on the Kettering-Cambridge line the station at Cranford would awake to the passage of the local iron ore trip from the truncated end of the branch at Twywell. It was here that wagons were loaded from tipper lorries backing up to an elevated ramp. It was purely by chance that this photograph was taken. Earlier in the afternoon on 12 May 1965, during a visit to Kettering shed, the photographer had casually asked what was happening to Stanier Jubilee No. 45660 ROOKE, which was unusually on shed. On being told it was working the Twywell trip he realized this was an opportunity not to be missed. Here we see 'Rooke' on the return journey with the loaded iron ore, easing its way through Cranford station, a far cry from racing along the main line with named expresses like 'The Devonian'. The station house is still in use as a private residence. *(Ken Fairey)*

147. Wednesday 2 May 1962, and Thrapston Bridge Street station witnesses the arrival of the 6 p.m. local train from Peterborough East to Northampton at 6.40 p.m. hauled by Stanier Black 5 No. 45301. This view from the level crossing shows the attractive station building, the outside of which was illustrated in an article on the opening of the line in *The Illustrated London News* on 14 June 1845. *(Tommy Tomalin)*

148. On this sunny morning at Thrapston Bridge Street station, escaping steam drifts around in the cold morning air as Stanier Black 5 No. 45398 awaits departure time on Friday 10 April 1964. The photographer joined this train at Ringstead and Addington station with his bicycle, leaving there at 7.49 a.m. for the short journey to Thrapston. 45398 remained a Northampton engine until the end of steam in 1965. *(Trevor Riddle)*

149. Springtime at Oundle on the Northampton to Peterborough line on Friday 10 April 1964 as Stanier 8F class 2-8-0 No. 48555 sets off with a freight train towards Northampton at 10.10 a.m. With the River Nene in the foreground and the landscape of Oundle in the background, the photographer has not only composed a superb picture, but has fired the camera shutter at the exact moment to capture the locomotive in the perfect position. Earlier, the freight train had pulled into the loop at Oundle station to allow the 9.45 a.m. Peterborough to Northampton train to pass. *(Trevor Riddle)*

TO THE MIDLAND LINE AND BEYOND

150/151. Peterborough Spital Bridge shed's ex-L.N.E.R. class B1 4-6-0 No. 61095, fitted with a self-weighing tender, rolls over the level crossing into Thrapston Bridge Street station looking immaculate in ex-works condition hauling the 9.32 a.m. from Northampton to Peterborough East on Saturday 6 June 1959. The passengers board the train and everybody patiently awaits the 10.12 a.m. departure time. Of interest is the ancient crane which was bedded on original stone slab sleepers from the London and Birmingham Railway. Another feature is the wagon turntable at the end of the siding, on which wagons could be turned at right angles and pushed into the goods shed. (*both pictures Ian L. Wright*)

152. Northampton-based Stanier class 5 No. 45050 travels effortlessly towards Northampton on a superb summer's evening on Monday 29 July 1963 with the 6 p.m. local from Peterborough East. It is 6.40 p.m. and the train has just departed from Thrapston Bridge Street station and passes the signalbox guarding the one-time Islip ironworks sidings. The photograph was taken from the Kettering to Cambridge line and the elevated position gives an excellent view of Thrapston in the background. *(Tommy Tomalin)*

TO THE MIDLAND LINE AND BEYOND

153. Stanier 8F No. 48609 bids farewell to Thrapston Midland as it leaves the station and crosses the viaduct with a freight bound for Kettering on Saturday 21 October 1961 – a scene that typifies the Kettering-Cambridge branch line's rural nature. The magnificent viaduct spanning the River Nene opened in 1866 when the first passenger trains began to run, and was almost 100 years old when the final goods traffic ended late in October 1963. The structure remained in situ for many years before finally being pulled down to make way for another new road scheme. *(Brian Denny)*

TO THE MIDLAND LINE AND BEYOND

154. On the very cold morning of Sunday 17 December 1961 a hoar frost decorates the meadows at Wellingborough as Ivatt tank No. 41278 works purposefully towards the bridge spanning the River Nene on the line between Wellingborough Midland Road and Wellingborough London Road stations. Unusually for a push-and-pull train the locomotive is running tender first while heading the 10.30 a.m. train to Northampton Castle station. Northampton-shedded 41278 was transferred to Llandudno Junction in July 1962 after 17 months at the shed. *(Tommy Tomalin)*

TO THE MIDLAND LINE AND BEYOND

155. Stanier Black 5 No. 45147 works hard through the winter landscape as it leaves Irthlingborough on a Peterborough East to Northampton local train during January 1959. The medieval bridge over the River Nene is seen in the left background. It carried the A6 road until bypassed in the late 1930s, but BR still operated the level crossing at Irthlingborough until final closure to goods trains in 1966. *(Ian L. Wright)*

156. As 45147 heads away, one sees just how bleak conditions were, with winter floods and frost in abundance, as the train makes for Wellingborough in this stunning winter landscape. Away in the right background the Richard Thomas and Baldwin 'Ebbw Vale' iron ore plant adds its vapours to the cold January air. 45147 was well known to local railwaymen as it had been at Northampton shed since 1948! *(Ian L. Wright)*

157. At Castle Ashby station on Saturday 23 December 1961 the weather was bright and sunny, but bitterly cold, when B1 class 4-6-0 No. 61236 arrived with the 9.28 a.m. train from Northampton Castle to Peterborough East. Here we see the train pulling strongly away from the station past a L.N.W.R. co-acting signal (where the same signal is at two different heights on the post) at 9.42 a.m. Co-acting signals were normally used where an obstructed view occurred, so one must assume there was originally a footbridge at Castle Ashby station, or one was proposed when the signal was installed. *(Tommy Tomalin courtesy Colour Rail)*

158. On the same day at Castle Ashby it is 10.20 a.m. and the peace is shattered once again as Stanier 8F No. 48492 pounds past Castle Ashby signalbox with wagon loads of South Wales coking coal bound for Corby steelworks. Castle Ashby station was originally named 'White Mills' when built by the LNWR, apparently after the stone mill that was situated on the River Nene nearby. The goods warehouse with its curved bottom canopy still stands and today is in use as a restaurant. *(Tommy Tomalin)*

TO THE MIDLAND LINE AND BEYOND

159. Locally shedded Stanier 8F 2-8-0 No. 48183 drifts through Wellingborough Midland Road Station with a freight train from the Midlands on Saturday 2 May 1964. The afternoon sunshine finds a gap between the station buildings to highlight the front of the locomotive as a young observer watches the train from the end of platform 1. Today the scene at Wellingborough is little changed, although the footbridge has been replaced with a modern version and all the semaphore signalling has disappeared. *(Roger West)*

160. The Locomotive Club of Great Britain organized a mammoth rail tour on Saturday 24 April 1965. Starting from St Pancras at around 8.30 a.m. it worked its way around Leicester, Nottingham, Mansfield, Skegness, Mablethorpe, Boston, back to Nottingham, Oakham, Wellingborough and back to St Pancras. In this excellent picture, which looks more like a painting than a photograph when projected on screen, we see the train at Wellingborough on the final leg of its journey. Various types of locomotive were used, this stage being hauled by Crewe North's immaculately turned out Britannia No. 70052 FIRTH OF TAY. With steam to spare and the blower on 'Firth of Tay' has its water tank replenished prior to leaving for St Pancras where it was due at 8.45 p.m. The cost of this tour was 63s (£3.15) for over 12 hours train travel. *(Ken Clements)*

To the Midland Line and Beyond

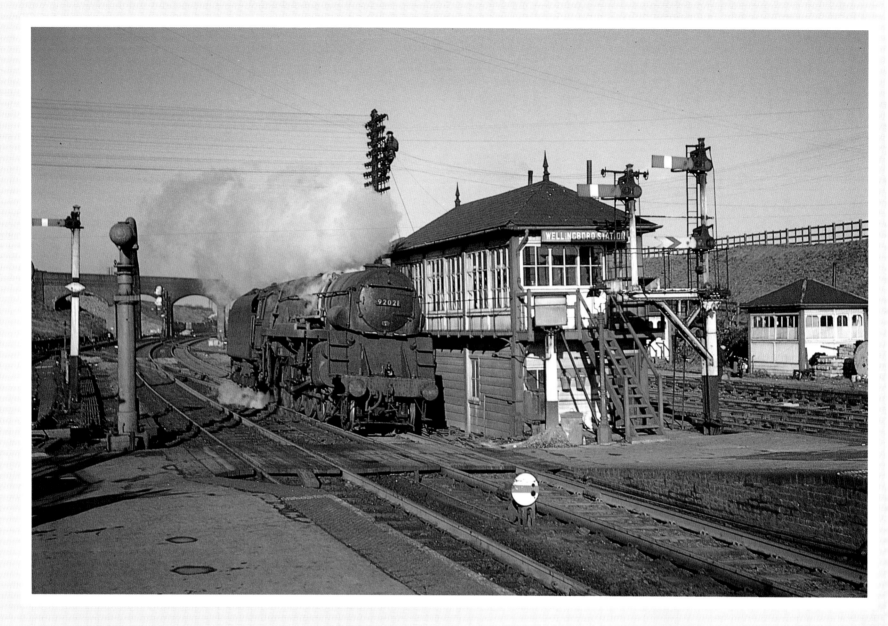

161. One of Wellingborough's ex-Crosti 2-10-0s No. 92021 scurries past Wellingborough's 48-lever signalbox on the up main line while making its way light engine from the shed to Wellingborough Midland Junction. It will then reverse and run down the Northampton-Peterborough line to Richard Thomas and Baldwin's Irthlingborough iron ore mine siding to pick up an iron ore train for Ebbw Vale in South Wales. Five or six trains left for South Wales each week travelling via Blisworth and Bletchley to Oxford where they were handed over to the Western Region for onward despatch via Didcot and Severn Tunnel Junction. These freight trains ceased to run when the R.T.B. mine closed in September 1966. On this sunny clear day early in 1961 the lineman on the telegraph pole hardly gives the Crosti a second glance. *(Ian L. Wright)*

162. A classic example of a 'Jubilee' hauling red coaches through Wellingborough Midland on the Midland main line. This view from the Mill Road bridge used to be a familiar sight to local enthusiasts as the expresses sped through. On this occasion an extremely clean Jubilee No.

45721 IMPREGNABLE heads northwards with a LCGB special on Sunday 6 June 1964. Numerous faces are peering out of this side of the coaches in anticipation of a view of Wellingborough loco shed, which is about to be passed the other side of the bridge. *(Robin Patrick)*

TO THE MIDLAND LINE AND BEYOND

163. Wellingborough shed yard viewed from 'Tipperary' sidings on a clear sunny evening during August 1964 finds a rather workstained Stanier Jubilee No. 45632 TONGA well away from its home shed of Stockport. In fact 'Tonga' spent most of its working life on the Western Division so must have been a rare visitor to Wellingborough. All the steam locomotives in view show signs of life as smoke and steam drift around in the evening atmosphere but, as can be seen, the diesel fleet was steadily increasing in numbers. *(Ken Clements)*

TO THE MIDLAND LINE AND BEYOND

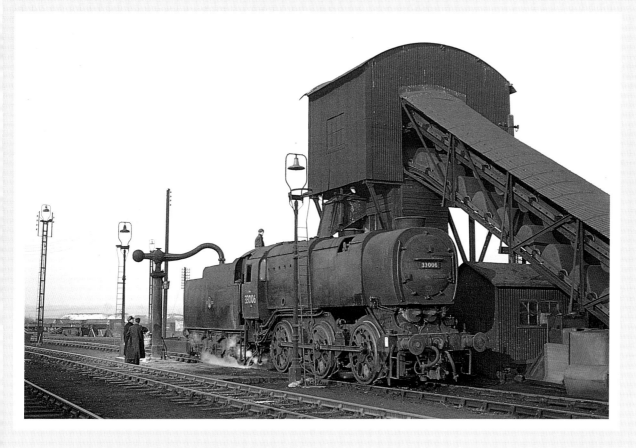

164. Wellingborough had some unusual locomotives visiting the shed during its time. On Sunday 7 March 1965 a Home Counties Railway Society railtour took place, hauled by two Southern locomotives, a U class No. 31639 and a Q1 class No. 33006. Starting at Paddington, the train travelled via Banbury, Stratford-upon-Avon, Rugby, Northampton, Wellingborough, Bedford, Bletchley, Oxford and back to Paddington. On reaching Wellingborough the locomotives had to be serviced and turned for the remaining part of the journey. Here we see No. 33006 having its water tank replenished while standing by the coaling plant at Wellingborough shed prior to hauling the train back towards Paddington with No. 31639. *(Ken Fairey)*

165. After a long haul down from Scotland, Highland Railway Jones Goods 4-6-0 No. 103 prepares to be serviced at Wellingborough Finedon Road before continuing its journey to Bedford on Thursday 7 May 1964. The reason for the visit was the 4-6-0's use in the film *Those Magnificent Men in their Flying Machines*, masquerading as a French Nord Railway 4-6-0, which was to be filmed on the Bedford to Hitchin branch. As the men busy themselves with No. 103, a Wellingborough ex-Crosti No. 92022 stealthily lurks behind the cabin. *(Ken Fairey)*

166. Another view of Wellingborough shed yard from 'Tipperary' sidings finds Wellingborough's splendid new Cowan, Sheldon 75-ton steam crane displayed with jib raised on Sunday 29 April 1962. Allocated BR No. RS1093/75, the crane remained at Wellingborough until August 1965, thereafter transferring to Cricklewood and eventual conversion to diesel power. Amongst the usual collection of work-worn Standard 9Fs, local resident No. 92134 raises steam ready for its next turn of duty. The low position of the sun also highlights a wheel-less ex-parcels van from one of the pre-grouping companies that was being used as a railwaymen's hut or store. (Sid Bellham)

TO THE MIDLAND LINE AND BEYOND

167. The winter sun beams into Finedon Road signalbox on Thursday 8 January 1987 while signalman Ron Griffin performs his duties with athleticism as he pulls off for another express train on the Midland main line. A permanent way worker takes a break from his duties and has come to have a chat and a mug of tea. Much pride was taken in the job, and everything was kept clean and tidy, including the frame which shines as it may have done the first day of use. Sadly, within a year the signalbox had closed and was later demolished. *(Joe Rajczonek)*

168. It's Christmas Eve 1962, and a low sun throws long shadows as Ivatt class 2-6-0 No. 43031 starts out of the sidings at Finedon Road signalbox with a long coal train heading for Brent in London. With a freezing easterly wind blowing and a gloriously clear winter light it's not surprising that frost on the track in the foreground has remained from the previous night. The crew will be only too pleased to get back home and start the Christmas celebrations rolling. Little did they realize what a bad winter was to follow! *(Sid Bellham)*

TO THE MIDLAND LINE AND BEYOND

169. The same train, having travelled under Finedon Road bridge, struggles to keep its load on the move, and slips occasionally on the icy rails as the sun glints off the boiler of the Ivatt, whilst in the foreground a fogman's hut stands prominent. *(Sid Bellham)*

170. Plumes of steam from the chimney of Wellingborough's 9F No. 92126 condense in the cold winter air of a February morning in 1963 as the locomotive powers through Wellingborough Midland Road station on the up slow line with a 'through freight' bound for the south. The dusting of snow and heavy frost linger on the platform and tracks as the temperature remains below freezing point despite the sun's presence. *(Ken Clements)*

171. In another winter landscape, this time at Irchester station on the main line to St Pancras, a Stanier 8F 2-8-0 No. 48381 struggles up Sharnbrook bank with a freight during January 1959, heading south on the more easily graded goods lines. Irchester's station buildings were unusually situated on the road bridge from where this photograph was taken. (*Ian L. Wright*)

TO THE MIDLAND LINE AND BEYOND

172. Ivatt 2-6-2 tank No. 41225 pauses briefly at Wellingborough London Road station with the 8.10 a.m. train from Northampton on Friday 1 May 1964. From Wellingborough London Road the train will climb up over the River Nene bridge to join the Midland main line at Wellingborough Midland Road station. The Ivatt 2-6-2 tanks were well liked by enginemen, and speeds in excess of 60 mph were regularly reached along the Northampton branch by some of the more enthusiastic drivers. (Ken Fairey)

TO THE MIDLAND LINE AND BEYOND

173. Long after passenger services ceased on the Higham Ferrers branch a railway society 'Brake Van Special' trundles through Rushden station on its way back to Wellingborough during Saturday 3 July 1965. Observed from the footbridge, Standard class 2 No. 78028 from Leicester shed works the special past the brick-built station buildings. 78028 was one of the class 2 Standards fitted with cut down mountings to allow for clearance in the narrow bore of Glenfield tunnel on the Leicester (West Bridge) branch. Fortunately Rushden station still stands and is the headquarters of the Rushden Historical Transport Society. *(Ken Fairey)*

The Higham Ferrers branch was 3½ miles long from its start at Irchester Junction on the Midland main line. The passenger trains were push-pull operated and ran over the goods lines between Wellingborough and Irchester Junction. Twelve trains ran each way on weekdays with three extra on Saturdays, the 11.57 a.m. S.O. being a class-5-hauled ten coach through train to Leicester.

174/175. In these two photographs a push-pull train arrives at Higham Ferrers behind Standard class 2 tank No. 84006 on the bright morning of 30 May 1959 just two weeks before closure to passenger services. A handful of passengers make their way onto the platform for a Saturday morning trip into Rushden or Wellingborough. The station was a stone built Midland Railway building which was nicely in character with the town. The line itself carried on into an extensive goods yard which terminated at the Kimbolton road. With both Higham Ferrers and Rushden being heavily involved in the shoe industry, the branch remained open to freight traffic for nearly ten years more. *(both pictures Ian L. Wright)*

TO THE MIDLAND LINE AND BEYOND

FROM QUARRY
TO STEELWORKS

176. HOLWELL No.30 built by Hawthorn Leslie in 1932 stands in Lodge Pit at Irchester, the green livery of the locomotive contrasting strongly with the coloured shades of the ironstone overburden. The photograph was taken on Friday 28 March 1968 15 months before the closure of the system. On this particular occasion there had been a power cut and the drag line bucket was stuck in the wagon. Alas no work was therefore possible and the locomotive returned to shed at 4 p.m. having remained idle all afternoon. This was particularly unfortunate as one of the authors (JR) and the photographer missed an afternoon at college to sample industrial steam for the first time in the county. That would teach us to miss lessons, or would it? *(Tony Haylock)*

177. Down in the depths of Desborough Quarry SHEEPBRIDGE No.27 waits to leave with a loaded train on Saturday 2 January 1965. The superb winter light helps the photographer to produce a really colourful photograph. The dragline in the background is removing overburden, and the ironstone strata is clearly visible. The photographer was fortunate to have a drive of the Hudswell Clarke locomotive on this occasion and therefore managed to gain access to the quarry. Engine crews were particularly friendly at quarry systems and an opportunity of a ride was regularly possible. Although the railway continued until December 1966 No. 27 was sadly scrapped in May of that year. *(Trevor Riddle)*

178. Viewed from near the Wellingborough to Wollaston Road on a February day in 1968, HOLWELL No. 30 pulls up the incline out of Lodge Pit, Irchester, making steady progress with its fully loaded ore wagons. The train is heading for the British Railway exchange sidings situated between Wellingborough Midland and Wellingborough London Road stations and is about to pass the quarry huts and workers' modes of transport parked in the adjacent field. (Ken Clements)

FROM QUARRY TO STEELWORKS

179. A walk up to Lodge pit at Irchester during April 1968 reveals an Andrew Barclay built locomotive No. 9 waiting impatiently to take its three wagons up the steep gradient to the BR exchange sidings. Unlike many other industrial quarry locomotives in the area No. 9 was black and lined yellow with yellow side rods and buffer beams. When the locomotive arrived from Lackeby about four years previously she carried the number 6 on cabside plates, but as Irchester already had a No. 6 locomotive the new arrival was altered to No. 9 by simply turning the plates upside down! When the quarry finally closed, No. 9 was preserved by the local Irchester Parish Council, and the locomotive ended up at the Wollaston Road recreation ground in August 1969. *(Ken Clements)*

180. With the discontinuation of Wellingborough No. 5 quarry in August 1964 No. 6 quarry was opened and ore was extracted from it for two years until the quarry system totally closed down. Narrow gauge Peckett-built locomotive No. 87, the largest of the three Pecketts at Wellingborough, can be seen coming out of No. 6 quarry with a loaded train on Tuesday 11 October 1966. On reaching Caroll Spring Farm sidings the locomotive would run round and work tender-first down the bank to Wellingborough. No. 87 was more powerful and heavier than the other two locomotives and the tendency was to use her on the main line where the track was better laid, and to use her advantage on the bank. She did, however, work in the pits when required, as in this picture. This locomotive is now preserved at the nearby Irchester Narrow Gauge Museum. *(Ken Fairey)*

181. All out effort as HOLWELL No. 17 drags its three wagons up the very steep incline out of Lodge Pit; Irchester, during a fine December's afternoon in 1967. The low setting sun has made the colour of the ironstone really stand out in the background as the locomotive leaks so much steam that it's almost enveloped as the last load of the day is brought to the exchange sidings. *(Ken Clements)*

FROM QUARRY TO STEELWORKS

182. A hot September's day, and Peckett locomotive No. 86 climbs up the steep bank with empty wagons on the mile branch line to Wellingborough No. 6 quarry and is about to cross the ungated Sidegate Lane crossing. This used to be a familiar site and sound for travellers on the road and a crossing keeper would normally come out of the shelter on the left armed with his red flags and wearing his white coat to halt the traffic. The train consists of four wagons, each loaded with two skips which can be lifted off once filled with iron ore. In the distant background Neilson's signalbox stands on the Midland main line adjacent to the BR wagon repair workshops. The scene was photographed on Tuesday 6 September 1966 during the last weeks of service before closure. *(Ken Fairey)*

183. Peckett-built 0-6-0ST No. 85 prepares to come onto shed at Wellingborough during September 1964 in the last week of operation. No. 85 was later preserved and today can be viewed at the Irchester Narrow Gauge museum in Irchester Country Park where it is steamed on occasions during the year. The spark arrester mounted on top of the chimney was necessary owing to the fire risk to the nearby cornfields. All other locomotives were similarly fitted. *(Ken Clements)*

184. A view of Wellingborough Ironworks from Nest Lane on Sunday 11 September 1960 shows WELLINGBORO' No. 5, built by Andrew Barclay in 1939, charging out from 'bogey hole' with slag lathes for tipping on the slag bank. The furnaces can be seen in the centre of the background with the wagon weighbridge on the left and the watering tank for steam locos on the right. In the summer months it was usual for the panel at the back of the locomotive to be removed so that it didn't feel quite so hot on the footplate. The status of the ironworks declined as the 1960s approached and although the two furnaces were in use during 1960 it was clear that the end was in sight. The falling demand for pig iron was responsible and the remaining furnace was blown out on 23 October 1962, and the works officially closed a week later after some 76 years in existence. *(Roger West)*

185. Having worked a Saturday morning stint Hudswell Clarke built 0-6-0ST locomotive of 1895 vintage stands outside the locomotive shed at Desborough on 28 March 1964 as the driver prepares the engine for lighting-up on the following Monday. Kindling wood is put around the smokebox to dry, then the coal bunker is filled, and finally the engine would have just enough steam remaining to allow the driver to back it into the shed. The 69-year-old veteran was being used during this period because another locomotive, HC 1695, had been damaged in a derailment, and an urgent order of 2,500 tons instead of the usual 1,800 tons had been placed. The locomotive was normally stored in the open and looks well work-stained. Of interest is the locoshed in the background with its extension made of asbestos and steel built next to the old brick locoshed. *(Roger West)*

186/187. Work is in full operation at the calcine bank at Five Willows sidings (this was known in production days as Five Willows Pit) during the summer of 1965 with No. 24, a Hudswell Clarke 0-6-0ST built in 1926, as the centre of attraction. Ore is loaded into removable skips placed transversely on a wagon frame, three per wagon, and taken back to the calcine bank where the skips are removed by a crane and emptied. Coal is then added so that the ironstone is burned to reduce impurities, weight and volume. Then the wagons are loaded again before transporting to the BR exchange sidings prior to shipment to steel works. In this view the calcine bank is visible with steam and smoke rising from the burning ore, the ore being in the skips behind the locomotive and the coal in skips in front of it. Calcining finally ceased at the end of December 1968 with the shutdown of Skinningrove ironworks. The last stocks of calcined ore were taken to Ketton Cement works by road up to the end of August 1969. No. 24 arrived here as late as the end of 1957 from Appleby Frodingham Steel Co, at Scunthorpe and continued to work until scrapped in May 1968. *(both pictures Trevor Riddle)*

188. Superb summer weather produces perfect conditions for colour photography at Cranford Quarry as LODDINGTON No. 2 sets off with a full load of ore on Monday 12 August 1968. The locomotive had arrived from the Loddington Quarry system some two years earlier, but had originally worked at Byfield Quarry until February 1965 where it received its first name BYFIELD No. 2. The quarry in view was due south of Cranford village and continued to be used until the end of June 1969 when the last ore was quarried. Cargo Fleet steelworks, Teesside, was to start using imported ore and so didn't require ore from Cranford any longer. A diesel locomotive was expected during the final six months of operation, but it never came and both LODDINGTON No. 2 and CRANFORD No. 2 reigned supreme right to the bitter end, with many photographers capturing the final months of operation on film. *(Robin Patrick)*

189. The epitome of quarry shed scenes as LODDINGTON No. 2 rests while its footplate crew have their mid-morning break on Whit Tuesday 27 May 1969. All the usual shed paraphernalia is gathered in the picture. The coal stage, the thrown down water pipe, the typical oil-caked floor, holes in the tin sheeting to the walls and doors, ash piles surrounding spring-green trees, the pit under the locomotive, wafting smoke from the built-up fire, the hissing injector, the shunting pole on the front of the locomotive and so on. No wonder this is one of the photographer's favourite pictures. What would one give to be there now? *(Roger West)*

190. A classic rural view of No. 24 once again hauling a train of freshly quarried ironstone at Cranford on Tuesday 4 June 1963. This delightful colour scene sums up the charming nature of the industrial railways as they used to be in the county. How pleasing that they were not totally neglected and photographs such as these were taken. In such pleasant summer conditions surely there was no more pleasant way to pass the time of day than to ride on and view these little green engines with their handful of ore laden wagons. Alas today the whole scene is under the A14 dual carriageway – such is progress! *(Roger West)*

FROM QUARRY TO STEELWORKS

191/192/193. Nassington Quarries, situated about two miles south of Wansford in the north-east of the county, had the honour of being the last ironstone quarry to use steam locomotives. Throughout their existence the quarries were worked almost entirely by two Hunslet locomotives that came in 1939/40. The loco-motives were named RING HAW and JACKS GREEN and were always kept in superb condition. Ring Haw was a piece of woodland alongside the Fotheringhay bridle way and a section of it was surrendered to ironstone as part of No. 2 quarry. Jacks Green was a small clearing in Great Byards Sale west of the Abethorpe bridleway. No. 3 quarry, featured in all three photographs, lay to the south of the BR line from Yarwell Junction to Rugby and was opened up in 1968, after BR had closed the line beyond the Nassington connection. Normal working practice at the time required one locomotive to be in the pit with wagons being loaded while the other would bring empty wagons from the BR exchange. As the line from the quarry to the BR line was very steep both locos would have to be used to return full wagons to the exchange sidings. All three pictures, taken on Wednesday 7 May 1969, show the crudely laid trackwork winding its way around the huge pile of overburden which, stained by various minerals, is mostly bias limestone and some 50-60 feet in depth. Raw ore continued to be quarried for another 18 months up until closure at the end of 1970, after which both of the locomotives were preserved. *(all pictures Robin Patrick)*

At the beginning of the 1960s some ten pits were in operation around the extensively quarried Corby area. As some closed, others were opened and Oakley pit was brought into production at the beginning of 1964. It was situated north-east of Great Oakley village and continued to be used until the final seven pits closed at the beginning of 1980. These pictures illustrate some of the operations taking place in Oakley pit on Friday 6 October 1967.

194. Locomotive No. 38 named DOLOBRAN, a Manning Wardle built in 1910, is being used on the platelayers' train. The quarry floor has been prepared for an extension of the track, and lengths of track are being unloaded and put into position. Note the striped revolving target in frame mounted on the lamp bracket of the locomotive. *(Roger West)*

195. An overhead view of No. 63, which arrived brand new in 1954 from the builders Robert Stephenson and Hawthorn Ltd, shows the driver going round his locomotive with the daily oiling pot in between duties. In the background the iron ore rock surface has been drilled ready for explosive charges to be mounted. In front of the locomotive on the track can be seen the pipe that carries the compressed air for drills. *(Roger West)*

196. 16-ton tipplers being loaded, with No. 63's safety valve ready to blow as the locomotive is prepared to move the train. The steep gradients out of the pit would normally require a locomotive at each end. No. 38 DOLOBRAN waits patiently in the background with the permanent way train having just arrived. The piles of overburden resemble a lunar landscape. *(Roger West)*

FROM QUARRY TO STEELWORKS

197. It is Saturday 25 March 1967; a splendid spring morning and traffic on the 'main line' is as busy as ever as a diesel-hauled train with sintered ore overtakes No. 62, a Robert Stephenson and Hawthorn-built locomotive, which is hauling a loaded train of ore from Cowthick quarry. The scene is viewed from the Stanion road bridge, and the iron ore is destined for the steelworks using BSC's internal tipplers as distinct from the BR 16-ton wagons. Cowthick quarry was situated south-east of Corby near Stanion village. Diesel locomotives gradually took over all operations, and steam ceased from January 1969, leaving only the steelworks' steam engines to operate for another two years. *(Roger West)*

FROM QUARRY TO STEELWORKS

198. A quite superb colour view of No. 47 CARNARVON bringing a loaded train of 30-ton tipplers out of Priors Hall pit on Friday 6 October 1967. This particular quarry was situated north-east of Corby between Deene and Little Weldon villages. As the quarry branches extended further east, and the overburden became heavier, there was usually a stiffish bank from the ironstone face to the 'main line' and the locos had to work hard. This was the case at Priors Hall where the gradient varied between 1 in 20 and 1 in 40 and the locomotives really thrashed along. The maximum load for one locomotive was eight tipplers, but in this illustration an extra one has been added. *(Roger West)*

199. A summer view of the exchange sidings at the Corby steelworks on Saturday 8 June 1963 shows yet another example of the fleet of S & L locomotives rubbing shoulders with Stanier 8F No. 48380 from Kettering shed. The latter shunts empty coal wagons while S & L No. 17 shunts tender first with slag ladles in the hot sunny weather. No. 17 was one of only two locomotives at Corby that carried a *side* tank instead of a *saddle* tank on its boiler. Footplate conditions on these small locomotives in this type of weather must have been particularly uncomfortable, especially on certain duties within the steelworks. *(Roger West)*

FROM QUARRY TO STEELWORKS

200. Victorian veteran No. 26, built by Andrew Barclay in Kilmarnock in 1890, sets off from the shed area within the steelworks complex after replenishment of coal and water. No mechanical coal loading facilities here, only the help of shovels to throw the coal into the locomotive's bunker. This particular locomotive arrived from Cadzow colliery in Scotland in 1945, and on this Saturday, 13 April 1963, was still being used regularly. *(Roger West)*

201. There's a hive of activity at Stewart & Lloyds sidings in Corby as oil burner No.15, one of the steelworks locomotives, arrives from the furnaces in the background with hot iron ladles, and begins to push them away round the curve to the right and onto the Bessemer. Meanwhile, Stanier 8F 2-8-0 No. 48288 shunts in the yard before collecting wagons from the sidings. On the grass bank opposite a group of children enjoy their Saturday morning's train-spotting on this spring day, 13 April 1963. *(Roger West)*

202. On Saturday morning 13 March 1971 sulphurous smoke belches out of Deene Coke ovens as red hot coke cascades into the coke car at Corby steelworks. Hawthorn Leslie 0-6-0 saddle tank No. 20 prepares to push the car under the quenching bay for cooling before discharging the coke down the slope in the foreground while returning past the ovens. At this time steam locomotives only worked the Lime Plant, Electric Furnace and Permanent Way, but owing to a diesel failure No. 20 was rostered to work Deene Coke ovens on this Saturday. *(Roger West)*

FROM QUARRY TO STEELWORKS

203. Sister Hawthorn Leslie saddle tank No. 21 is rostered on a 'Furnace Front' job in place of another unavailable diesel on Saturday 30 January 1971. No. 21 is seen from Rockingham Road bridge during this miserable wet day pushing a line of slag bogies, the only bright spot in the overcast gloom being the fire hole in the locomotive's cab. The loaded slag bogies will be pushed to the Tarmac plant some 1^1/$_2$ miles away. There was said to be 102 miles of track at Corby steelworks. No. 21 was the last of the steelworks steam locomotives and worked for the final time on 26 June 1973 hauling an enthusiasts' train. (Roger West)

Access to the rail system within the Corby steelworks complex was impossible without permission and, with the plant being very busy all round the clock, visits were not encouraged for safety reasons. However, on this occasion on Friday 4 October 1963 the photographer managed to gain access, and here are two illustrations showing the kind of conditions experienced.

204. Another oil burning locomotive, No. 12, a Hunslet built in 1934 (in its distinctive yellow livery to make it stand out within the steelworks) poses between shunting duties. In the background two diesel locomotives can be seen at work, while acrid fumes are released into the air and fill the sky creating an industrial atmosphere unique to this type of environment. (Roger West)

205. In another part of the works there is yet more industrial atmosphere as locomotive No. 40, a Hunslet built in 1919 and used for 34 years in the steelworks, appears from inside the Bessemer building extremely work-stained and hauling ladles filled with red hot slag. One can almost feel the heat from the ladle and smell the choking smoke as the locomotive squeals round the bend amid all the scrap metal and grime associated with this part of the works. A picture that really sums up how Corby steelworks and its steam locomotives played a part in the county's railway history – in the good old days of steam! *(Roger West)*

FROM QUARRY TO STEELWORKS

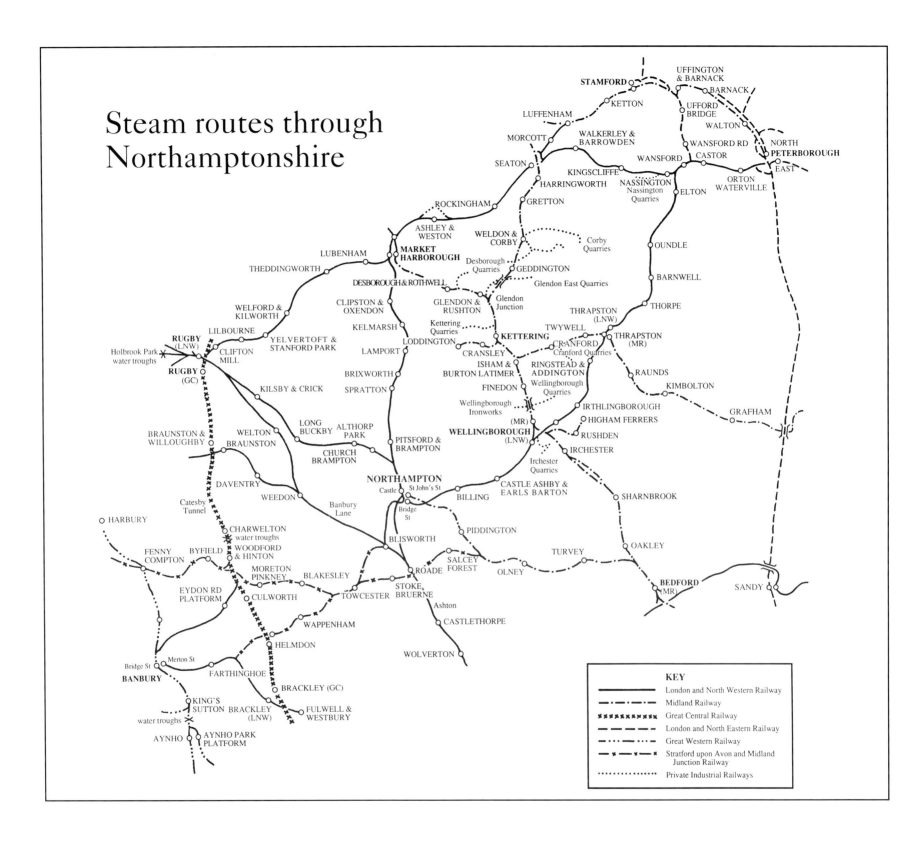

Steam routes through Northamptonshire

KEY

London and North Western Railway
Midland Railway
Great Central Railway
London and North Eastern Railway
Great Western Railway
Stratford upon Avon and Midland Junction Railway
Private Industrial Railways

INDEX OF LOCOMOTIVES

Having deposited a freight train earlier in the day at Far Cotton goods depot in Northampton, Bedford 3F No. 43766 heads towards home with its solitary brake van on 7 January 1961, having just passed Turvey station. *(Brian Denny)*